BOB JONES' REVIVAL SERMONS

Bob Jones'

REVIVAL SERMONS

By

1883

EVANGELIST BOB JONES, D.D., LL.D.

Founder Bob Jones University,
Greenville, South Carolina

Author of *Things I Have Learned*, and *Here and Hereafter*

SWORD OF THE LORD PUBLISHERS
Wheaton, Illinois

44.777

CONTENTS

DR. BOB JONES, SR., has been in revival work for half a century, having held his first revival campaign in a brush arbor when he was fifteen years old! He has preached to more people, taken more part in revival campaigns, seen more people take Christ as Saviour than any other man living. Although he was an evangelistic contemporary of R. A. Torrey, Billy Sunday, Gipsy Smith, and William Biederwolf, he is still going strong, seeing thousands saved yearly in great revival campaigns. To the vigor of his thought and the power of his preaching, the reader will testify.

These sermons were preached in a city-wide revival campaign sponsored by some two hundred churches in the Chicago Arena, April 28 to June 2, 1946. Attendance reached approximately six thousand. Since Dr. Jones preached the first two weeks of a five-week campaign (followed by Dr. Paul Rood and the writer of this introduction), these messages are laying the ground work for the campaign, reviving the saints, arousing interest, bringing conviction, and preparing the way for a blessed ingathering. Many were turned to God under the power of these messages.

I am somewhat familiar with the printed sermons of great preachers. I heard Dr. George W. Truett many times during his prime. I have heard Scarborough, Philpott, Gipsy Smith, Sunday and Rader. He has something of the earnestness of Truett, the story-telling charm of Rader, the sweet simplicity of Gipsy Smith, the courageous convictions of Billy Sunday. I thank God that we can now have in print some of the old-time revival sermons by Dr. Bob Jones, Sr. Un-.counted thousands have been moved by them, changed by them, blessed by them. May they burn anew in the heart of every reader!

JOHN R. RICE
Wheaton, Illinois

Chapter 1

FOLLOWING JESUS

"And as Jesus passed forth from thence, he saw a man, named Matthew sitting at the receipt of custom: and he saith unto him, Follow me. And he arose, and followed him."—Matthew 9:9.

*Y*OU WILL NOTICE that this is a personal invitation given by our Lord to Matthew. But the invitation to follow Jesus has pressed its way down the years and is extended to everybody in this building tonight. Of course, we use this in a figurative sense. You cannot follow Jesus Christ literally. Sometimes people say, "What would Jesus do?" You remember that very popular book in this country which expressed that sentiment, *In His Steps*. I would not discount it. The sentiment was beautiful. The idea of the book is, "What would Jesus do under certain circumstances? What would Jesus do if He were here just as I am?"

I am speaking reverently tonight. Did you ever stop to think that you have problems to solve which Jesus did not have to solve? Jesus was not a married man. Jesus was not a mother. Jesus did not live in Chicago. Jesus did not transact business in the complex business world in which you and I are living. Jesus Christ never traveled by automobile. Jesus Christ never went up in a plane. I am speaking reverently when I say that you have problems He did not have to solve. So the big question is not what would Jesus do. The big question is this: "Do I possess Jesus and does Jesus possess me?" If I possess Him and He possesses me, then under all circumstances in life I will do just what I ought to do. Every relationship will be right. I will be the right kind of father, the right kind of husband, the right kind of wife, the right

9

kind of mother, the right kind of citizen, the right kind of employee, the right kind of man or woman. Every relationship will be right if I am under the control of Jesus Christ.

Down in Alabama years ago I knew a man and a woman who had been married for fifty years. The man was unusually small and a blond. His wife was extremely large and a brunette. But that man and that woman actually looked alike. I used to look into his eyes and see an expression that made me think of the eyes of his wife. I used to look into her face and see features that reminded me of the face of her husband. For fifty years this man and this woman had gone life's way together. They had spent Christmas holidays together. They had been on picnics together. They had been up at the hour of midnight about the bedside of a sick child together. They had gone to the cemetery together to bury some of their children and had come back home to mingle their tears together. For fifty years their lives had been so mixed and mingled and blended until she had in her life a part of the life of her husband, and he had in his life a part of the life of his wife. If two human beings may commune until they become like each other, may not you and I commune with Jesus Christ until we, to some extent at least, become like Him?

Paul understood this when he reached mature old age. He looked from his dismal prison cell and said, "For to me to live is Christ, and to die is gain." Jesus Christ, seated at the right hand of the Father, is, to some extent at least, reproducing His life in the life of every consecrated, godly Christian man or woman.

When Were You Converted?

Do you remember when you were converted? Some of you know the time and the place. Let me stop just a minute to say that you do not have to know the time and place, but you had better be dead sure there was a time and you had better be dead sure there was a place.

A man said to me not long ago, "I do not believe in instantaneous conversion." There is no other kind of conversion but instantaneous conversion. You may not know when it happened, but if you are a Christian it did happen. You may not know just the second it took place, but if you are a Christian there was a moment in your life when you stepped out of darkness into light and out of death into life. You may have gradually come up to the line, but there was a moment when you stepped over; and if you did not step over you are still a sinner. You are dead in trespasses and sin. You do not have to know just when you were saved, but you had better be dead sure you are saved.

A great preacher said to me, "I do not know just when I was converted. Sometimes the Devil comes to me and says, 'You cannot tell when it happened.' And I say to him, 'Well, then, I will claim Him right now as my Saviour!'"

Some of us remember the time and the place. With some of us it is the memory of a church altar in the old home town. With some of us it is the memory of what we call the "mourners' bench," in some church down South. With some of us it is the memory of the old family altar where our fathers led in prayer. With some of us there may be the memory of the old barnyard back at the old country home. With some of us there may be the memory of a lonely spot where we met God for the first time under the starlit sky of midnight. But some of us remember the time and place. There was that moment when everything became new, and we saw as we had never seen before; we heard as we had never heard before; we felt as we had never felt before. God did that for us in a moment. Say, if God can do that for a man in a moment, what cannot God do for men who will live surrendered lives for ten or twenty-five or fifty consecrated years? If God can so transform in a second, what could not God do in a lifetime if given a chance!

Listen, we read in the Bible that the hour of prayer had come. Peter and John started to the temple to pray. They had been through the most wonderful epoch in the history of the world. They had gone through the lonely hours when Jesus hung on the cross. They had gone through the lonely days when His body was in the sepulcher. They had gone through the glorious manifestation when He came out of the tomb. They had had fellowship with Him this side of the grave. They had gone through that glorious experience when they saw Him climb an invisible stairway back to the sky. They had gone through that glorious manifestation when cloven tongues of fire came down at Pentecost.

Do You Keep Your Dates with God?

Now there they were—these men going along at the hour of prayer on their way to a prayer meeting. Say, they had kept a date with God. Do you keep your dates with God? You have a date with Him to read your Bible every day. Do you keep it? You have a date with Him to meet Him in prayer in some place of fellowship. Do you meet Him? At prayer meeting every week you have a date with God. Have you been keeping it?

The hour of prayer had come and Peter and John had started to the temple to pray. They said, "We have a date with God; it is time to go." They got to the gate of the temple and found a poor, crippled man who had never walked. He lifted his trembling hand and asked them for money. They said, "We do not have any money, but we have something better than money. We will fix you up so you can make some money." That is the best charity in the world. One of them reached out his hand, and the poor cripple got hold of it. He got on his feet and found he could stand alone. Then he went on into the temple, leaping and bounding and praising God. Are you surprised? Suppose you had never walked in your life. Suppose you had been sitting at the gateway of this building tonight, a poor, helpless cripple. Suppose other people had been walking by and you could not walk. Then suppose somebody helped you get on your feet. Suppose somebody said, "Now you can walk." Don't you think you would have come into this building leaping and bounding and praising God?

Some of us remember when we made our first step heavenward. One day Jesus passed. His brow was pierced with many a thorn. He came by. We looked up at him as He said, "Wouldn't you like to walk?"

We said, "We can't walk. Every time we get up we fall down. We are poor, crippled people."

He said, "I will fix you so you can walk." He reached out His nail-pierced hand.

I got hold of that hand one day. That hand that made all worlds gripped my hand. He pulled me to my feet. Eternal life and victory swept through my soul, and I made my first step toward Heaven. I did not shout. You may think I am excitable, but my pulse just beat sixty times a minute. I am very intense but not very excitable. I have never shouted in my life, but I wonder how a fellow could be a Christian and not shout. I have thought of it a thousand times. To stop and think what it means to walk the shining road with the Son of God to a cloudless sky is enough to make men shout!

Men shout over everything else. In this Arena men have shouted. Games have been held here when men went wild with excitement. A man can make a safe run home on a baseball diamond and the crowd shouts over the victory, and nothing is said about it. On the street corner is a group of men. One of them tells a joke and they mingle their shouts of laughter, and there is nothing said about it. Some folks are in the country at a picnic. It is a day of rest and pleasure. Young folks stroll down through the forest. One of them plucks a beautiful flower near a rippling stream and sends up a shout of laughter. Nothing is said about it. A little child looks down the street and sees his daddy coming. He claps his hands with glee and shouts and says, "Daddy is coming!" And there is nothing said about it.

But a wayward, ruined sinner with his back on Heaven and his face toward Hell, groping his way through the darkness of time to eternal night, feels about him in the gloom until he gets hold of the hand of Jesus. When he feels that touch he says, "Hallelujah! Glory to God!"

And somebody says, "Don't get excited, brother!"

We applaud men when they come home, scarred from battle. We applaud men when they are elected to office. We applaud men when they win athletic contests. But the angels applaud men when they come to God. Over the battlements of Heaven right now the angels look down on this Arena. They say, "Yonder is a sinner. Don't you hope he will come to Jesus? See that boy back yonder? His mother has been praying for him. That other fellow back there has a mighty good Christian wife. That girl over there has a good, sweet Christian mother. Wouldn't it be wonderful if she should come?" They listen over the battlements to the preacher. Then after a while the invitation is given, and some sinner starts down the aisle. The angels burst out saying, "Give him a hand! Give him a hand!" They lean over the battlements of the sky and applaud. It is wonderful to be a Christian. It is wonderful to keep step with Jesus Christ up this shining road.

Miraculous Cure

We read in the Bible about a woman who had a disease of the blood. She had tried all the doctors. She had been to the homeopaths, the allopaths, the osteopaths, the chiropractors and all the rest of them. I imagine she spent her time telling about her doctors and her operations. She had tried all the doctors and had about given up. But one day somebody said, "There is one Doctor who can make you well if you can ever get in touch with Him. I have seen Him unstop deaf ears and make a man hear. I saw Him open blind eyes and make a man see. That Doctor chased leprosy away with His touch. That Doctor can cure the palsied. There are no hopeless cases when He is around. He can actually raise the dead. When He goes around dead folks get up out of their coffins!"

The woman said, "If He ever comes to my town I believe I will try Him."

One day somebody said to her, "Have you heard the latest? The Doctor is in town!"

She said, "Is He really here?"

"Yes, He is here."

"I believe I will see if I can get in touch with Him," she said.

I imagine she told her friends that she wanted to go. They said, "You had better stay away from all that excitement down there in that Arena. I would not have anything to do with it!"

She said, "Well, I am in a bad fix anyhow. It can't be much worse with me than it is, and I think I will try it." I think she got up and began to dress. In my imagination I can see her now. I think she might have been nervous, trembly and maybe a little irritable and sensitive. After a while she said, "Goodby, children. I am going downtown and see if I can do anything for myself."

She started down the street, stopping once in a while to lean on her cane. A little later she saw a great crowd. She said, "He is in that crowd somewhere. I don't know how I will ever get to Him, but I am going to try!" And, listen! Nobody ever wanted to get to Jesus but that there was a way to Him. You may have to sail bloody seas and scale the mountains and climb over walls and go through bayonets and fields sown with dragon's teeth; but if you want to get to Him you can.

I see her as she approached the crowd and began to press her way through. One person and then another let her by. I think I see her as she put her trembling hand on the shoulder of an old fellow and said, "Mister, won't you let me by?"

He was hard and coarse, but he looked at her in pity and said, "Yes, come on by."

She came up to a little girl and said, "Honey, won't you let me see if I can't get to Him just to touch Him?" The little girl stepped out of the way.

After a while she got as close as she could get—but that is as close as anybody has to get to Jesus, just as close as he can. She took her cane and put it in her other hand. I think I can see her as she trembled for just a moment and said, "I will see if I can reach Him." She reached over and just touched His garment with her fingertip and stood back sound and well! Do you suppose she ever forgot that touch? She is probably talking about it in Heaven tonight. She is no doubt telling the angels and the redeemed about it.

Get Close to Jesus

You can get closer to Jesus than to touch His garment. You can touch Him, Himself. Right in front of you tonight is a nail-pierced hand. If you want to you can reach up and get it. You can grip it and it will grip you. You can sing the song, "Where He leads me I will follow." You can say, "It may be over mountains and across plains, but I will go with Him all the way."

"Oh," you say, "Bob Jones, that sounds good." Well, buddy, it is better than it sounds! No poet who ever wrote music could tell you how wonderful it is.

"But," you say, "I can't understand it." You do not have to understand it. That is the beauty of it. When I came to Jesus Christ I did not know what the words *vicarious* and *substitutional* meant. I did not know theological terms. I was an eleven-year-old country boy. All I knew was that God loved me and Jesus died for me and wanted to save me. I got to Him, and ever since that time I have been studying the wonders and the glory and the explanation of it. I did not understand it then. You do not have to have much sense to be a Christian. (That ought to be a lot of comfort to some of you!) Did you ever stop to think that you do not have to have much in your head to be a Christian? You just have to have a willing heart. You do not have to understand how food is digested to eat food and get nourishment. You do not have to understand how medicine cures. All you need to do is to get the medicine. You do not have to understand everything in the Bible. I have a lot of things I am going to ask Jesus about when I get to Heaven. There are some things in the book of Revelation I have never quite understood. There are some things in the book of Daniel that I have never quite understood. There are some marvelous things all through the Bible about which I have wondered and prayed. But there is one thing that is as clear as the light of the clearest noonday, and that is the road to Heaven. That road is well marked. You do not have to miss it. There may be some mysteries connected with the road, but the road itself is clear and definite and you do not have to miss it. If you want to know how to go to Heaven—Jesus is the way. Do you want to know how to go to Heaven? If you do, come to Jesus and trust Him—that is all. Do you want to know how to be saved? Look to Jesus to save you—that is all.

> Just as I am, without one plea,
>   But that Thy blood was shed for me,
> And that Thou bidd'st me come to Thee,
>   O Lamb of God, I come! I come!

Listen! I have never seen a man lost because of his inability to understand. You talk about "honest doubters." Jesus Christ settled that question forever. He said, "If any man will do his will, he shall know of the doctrine, whether it be of God or whether I speak of myself."

Do you know what the trouble with you is? You are not willing to pay the price. It is not a popular thing to be a Christian. There never has been a time since Jesus Christ died on Calvary when it has been a popular thing to be a Christian. It is not a popular thing in Chicago. Oh, it may be popular to be a church member, but it is not popular and never has been popular to be a Christian.

Not Popular to Be a Christian

I remember when I started in the ministry a young man said, "Bob, are you going to be a preacher?"

I answered, "Yes."

"Are you going to preach the truth?" he asked.

I said, "If I know it."

He said, "You won't be popular."

I said, "What are the smiles of men worth? They will vanish like morning clouds and float away like bubbles on the stream."

What does it matter what the world thinks of you? What does it matter? You live today; tomorrow you die; the next day you are buried; the next day you are forgotten. Listen! Isn't a man a fool who would go back on God for the smiles of a world that would not miss him if he were dead?

Popularity! Somebody said to me about a certain man: "He hasn't an enemy on earth."

I said, "He is no good!"

You cannot move without producing friction, and you cannot stand for Jesus Christ without producing friction. The world was not against Jesus Christ because He was bad. The world was against Him because He was good and the world was bad. People tried to make Him bad and drag Him to the low level on which they lived. And when He was tried in court the judge said, 'I can't find anything against Him.'

Because they could not find anything against Him they put Him on a cross. The world is against everybody who lines up on the side of Jesus Christ.

I was talking to my banker, a fine Christian man, the other day. He said, "Dr. Bob, why is it that some people will curse a good Christian school like Bob Jones University and other Christian colleges? Why are people against them? The young people in them are decent, clean and fine. They do not drink and smoke and gamble and swear. Why on earth are people against Christian colleges?"

I said, "Brother, the Devil is not against a bank. The Devil is not against a grocery store. The Devil is not against a dry goods store. The Devil is against a Christian testimony. If you were to put a sign out in front of this bank which would say to this wicked world, 'This bank stands without apology for the blood of Jesus Christ. This bank stands without apology for salvation by grace through faith in the atoning blood of Jesus,' you would line up all the demons against your bank."

The moment you step over on the side of Jesus Christ, that moment you line up wicked men against you.

Popularity! Popularity!

I remember a woman in the South once said to me, "Mr. Jones, I have such a lovely daughter. She is very popular. I do not know why she is so popular." I did not tell her that I did not understand it either—I had already seen her!

The meeting we were in went on for a few days, and one day the mother of that very popular girl came to the front. She found God. After she found God she looked up to me and said, "I want you to help me save my daughter. I must get her converted." I could not resist the impulse; I said, "You have been ambitious for her worldly position. You have pushed her into society. You have pushed her so far that I am afraid we cannot reach her."

The campaign closed and the girl was left in her worldliness and frivolity without God. Two years later I lectured in a town near there. When I came from the stage in the opera house a girl with a prematurely old face—the kind of face that a girl should not have, a face that was tired and worldly and worn and unhappy—came down the aisle. She said to me, "Do you remember me?"

I said, "Why, yes, Miss Annie. How are you getting along?"

"Oh," she said, "Just the same."

"Are you still a sinner?"

"Yes, I suppose I am a hopeless case."

There are mothers in Chicago who would rather see their daughters popular in society than to see them have front seats in Heaven. The reason some folks do not walk with Jesus Christ is that they would rather travel with the crowd.

One day a woman said to me, "I would like to be a Christian, but if I were to come down the aisle of this tabernacle and take a stand and accept Jesus Christ, I would have to give up my crowd."

I said, "No you wouldn't."

"Oh," she said, "I would."

I said, "No, you would not. If you were to walk down this aisle and take Jesus Christ as your Saviour and come out on His side without any apology, that godless, good-for-nothing, frivolous gang would give you up and save you the trouble." You do not have to give the world up; the world drops you when you step on Jesus' side. But I would rather be with Him who is not so fickle. I would rather walk alone with Him than to travel with the crowd to Hell!

Popularity! Popularity!

Fame Is Brief

I have seen in my lifetime the men whose names have been famous in my day. I remember when I was a boy we heard one day about William Jennings Bryan's capturing a convention. Not long ago I was in Washington and went out to the Arlington Cemetery where the dust of Bryan sleeps. The man at the cemetery told me that more people ask for Bryan's grave than any grave in the cemetery except the grave of the Unknown Soldier. I have seen Bryan still the thousands with his eloquence. I saw him in New York during the last Democratic Convention he ever attended. I sat in the gallery amid hissing, mocking hoodlums when they said, "The old man has reached the age of toothless senility." I saw him stand there and with eloquence I had rarely ever heard hush that crowd into silence and respect.

But William Jennings Bryan is dead and sleeps the sleep of death in a silent tomb. He used to stir the hearts of millions. But how long has it been since you thought of him? When did you ever think of Bryan? He has been dead only a few years.

I could mention others. I could talk to you about William McKinley. I was in Ohio recently in his home city. I said to somebody, "How long has it been since you thought of Mc-

Kinley?" I remember when he died. I was a country boy in Alabama. I remember how we unfurled the flag and how we wept to think a good president was dead. When did you think of him? He has been dead a little while, but when did you think of him?

Let's call the roll of others. There was Teddy Roosevelt, the "irresistible Teddy," the "Big-Stick Teddy," that man who shook a continent when he walked! But he is dead. He died from an infection and sleeps the sleep of death with other teeming millions who used to live, too. When did you ever think of him?

Think of Woodrow Wilson, who for a little while probably rose to higher heights of fame than any man in human history. For a little season the name of Woodrow Wilson stirred hope in the hearts of men as few names have ever stirred. I was in Washington recently and visited the cathedral. I said, "Oh, this is his tomb."

They said, "No, that is not his tomb. That is just a marker. He is buried in a secret place of the cathedral. He is not here; that is just a marker."

Wilson is dead. When did you think of him last?

I could call the roll of others. Think of Franklin Roosevelt, the man we said was indispensable; the man we said the world could not run without. He died. You can hear his voice now in memory saying, "My friends, . . ." He was the man who seemed unbeatable, and yet he is dead. You do not think of him very often now. In a few years you will not think of him at all.

Homer Rodeheaver told me the other day, "Bob, it is the strangest thing in the world; I can go into high schools in this country and ask the students in those schools, 'How many of you ever heard of Billy Sunday?' and scores and scores of them never ever heard of Billy Sunday, that man whose name in the religious world was a household word in this country."

Listen! People will not remember you until you get cold! If you died tonight, in thirty-six hours we would put you to bed with a shovel and cover you up with dirt and forget you. And yet some of you here tonight will turn your back on Jesus Christ for a world like that.

Do you know why you do not go with Him? You do not want to give up sin.

Now get this straight: giving up sin never saved anybody. Sins are simply limbs on the tree of sin. Sawing off limbs does not get rid of the tree of sin. Quitting a bad habit does not save a sinner. It is not what you give up that saves you; it is what you get when you take Jesus that saves you. It is not giving up something; it is getting something that saves people. Get that straight!

Christ Must Be First

But at the same time remember that you cannot have Jesus Christ as long as you have a sin you had rather have than to have Him. I am sick and tired of this superficial sort of Christianity we have in this country! If you want Jesus Christ, you must want Him more than you want anything or you will not have him! You cannot have anything in preference to Him. "Thou shalt have no other gods before me." Your god is the thing that is first in your life. If you have something else that is first, you cannot have Jesus. You must put Him first. You will notice that the Scripture did not say, "You must not have a bad god." You must not have *any* god, not even a good god. If your church is first with you, you are a sinner. If your lodge is first with you, you are a sinner. If your wife is first, you are a sinner. If your baby is first, you are a sinner. The only man who is a real saint is the man who puts Jesus first. JESUS FIRST!

Years ago when I was a young preacher I was holding a meeting in a town in the South. I was staying in a little hotel in the town. There was a lovely little girl about sixteen years old there. She had big black eyes. I never saw a girl her age with as much pep. She would blow in that house like a cyclone. She was all over the place, and she was irresistible in her magnetism and personality. I like folks like that. Deliver me from people who have nothing to them. I do have some respect for the prodigal son. He made a bad record, but he did make a record! I like folks who have something to them. I like to see folks like that saved.

That girl would come to the services. She did not care a thing about my preaching, but she liked to see me sweat. And she enjoyed the singer's pep. I used to watch her big, black eyes beam.

One night the Holy Ghost got hold of her. Oh, when He gets hold of people! I could see her as she began to cry. I just keep pouring it into her soul. When I finished I said to the people, "If you want to be saved, come to the front." She did not wait for anybody else; she led the procession. Down the aisles the people began to come after her. I went and sat down by her. She was crying the biggest tears, I think, I ever saw. I said, "Do you want to be saved?"

She said, "Mr. Jones, I—I—don't see any harm in dancing."

I said, "I haven't said a word about dancing. You ought to trust Jesus."

She said, "But I don't see any harm in dancing."

I said, "Wait a minute. Who is talking about dancing? Why are you bringing up that subject?"

"Well, I don't see any harm in it," she said again.

"Well, what are you worrying about?" I said. "I am not talking to you about that. I want to know if you will trust Jesus."

"Well, I don't see any harm in dancing."

Do you know what was the matter with that girl? She had been to one or two little dances at the town hall. She had smelled the perfume of the flowers. She had heard the music go out over the air. She had had the thrill of the whirl, and that night Jesus looked at her and said, "Which, which—that or Me?"

She said, "I want you, Jesus; but I want that, too."

Jesus said, "Which—that or Me?"

She said, "I want—I want You, Jesus; but I want that."

Jesus said, "You will have to choose tonight. You must put one or the other first in your heart. Which is it?"

Does Anything Keep You from Jesus?

That is the issue in your case. Now, don't misunderstand me. Do not misquote me! I do not say that everybody who dances goes to Hell. I say—and I will meet you at the judgment seat of Christ on it—if the dance keeps you from Jesus Christ, the dance will send your soul to Hell. Anything that keeps a man from Christ will damn him, whatever it is. If it is a shop or a store, or gold or cards—or anything else that keeps you from Jesus Christ—it will damn you. If you want Jesus you must want Him more than you want anything else, or you cannot have Him.

Let me tell you another story quickly. Years ago in a meeting down South I said, "If anybody here wants to be saved, come up to the front. Jesus can save you." A great many people came, and down the aisle with the others there staggered the bumiest old bum I think I ever saw. His hair was matted with dirt. His eyes were bloated and bloodshot. His clothes were ragged. His body was vermin-infested and dirty.

I am always happy to see an old bum saved, but I am so glad God saved me before I got to be a bum. And I am going to be honest with you: it was never easy for me to put my arm around a dirty person. I think there is a lot of good, old-time religion in a soap and rag. The first thing any bum in this town who is converted will do is to take a bath. I haven't any confidence in any man's Christianity who does not take a bath when he ought to have it.

The old dirty, filthy bum knelt at the front; and I thought, "I could have been just like him if my father had not taken me to a revival when I was eleven years old."

There were a lot of nice, decent people kneeling, too; but

I went over and put my arm around the old bum and said, "Do you want to be saved?"

I can see him now as he looked out of those bleared, blood-shot eyes and said, "Do you think Jesus could do anything for me?"

I said, "Yes, sir, Jesus can save you."

"Well," he said, "you s—s—ee, I—I'm an old drunkard."

I said, "Jesus can save an old drunkard."

"Well," he said, "You know, I've been a drunkard for thirty-seven years."

I said, "Jesus can save a man who has been a drunkard for thirty-seven years."

He said, "J—just a m—m—inute. I—I was thinking about it back there tonight when you were talking. I d—d—don't believe there has been one day in ten years that I have been sober."

I said, "Jesus can save a man who has been drunk for ten years."

"Well," he said, "j—j—just a m—m—oment. I s—s—up-pose y—y—ou've noticed that I am slightly intoxicated to-night."

I said, "Jesus can save a man who is drunk tonight! Will you trust Him as your Saviour?"

He looked at me for a moment. I saw a little expression of restored manhood come to his bloodshot eyes. He lifted his trembling hand above his head for a moment. Then he let it fall on the bench. He said, "I'll die before I'll ever touch another drop! Save me, Jesus; save me now!" Then he said, "You know, I'm saved." I did not even have to tell him; the Lord told him. He said, "I want to join the church right away." I did not know but one church represented there that could take him in on the spot and that was a Methodist church. A Methodist preacher was standing there. I said, "What church do you want to join?"

He said, "My wife is a Methodist." I called the preacher

over to where we were. He took him to one side, gave him the vows of membership and took him into the Methodist church. I kept up with him. He lived a sober, triumphant, victorious, witnessing Christian life for seven long years and died a triumphant, victorious death and shouted his way home to God.

Listen! Any man who wants Jesus above everything else can have Him and get victory the moment he wants Him like that.

No Easy Place on Road to Heaven

"Oh," you say, "Bob Jones, it is hard after you start." That is right. If there is any easy place on the road to Heaven, I have not reached it yet.

> Must I be carried to the skies
> On flowery beds of ease
> While others fought to win the prize
> And sailed through bloody seas?

"We wrestle not against flesh and blood, but against principalities, against powers, against the rulers of the darkness of this world, against spiritual wickedness in high places." "Put on the whole armour of God." Get ready for battle!

A man said to me, "The Devil has not bothered me for over ten long years."

I said, "Brother, I wouldn't tell that. A man is mighty sorry when the Devil doesn't want him." The Devil hounded the steps of Jesus Christ for all the years of His earthly life, and you are going to have to face all Hell when you start. But you do not have to fight alone. The One who was always victorious can give you victory. Everybody ever born into this world was challenged by the Devil, and he knocked out everybody who ever went into the ring with him. He knocked out Abraham. He knocked out Moses. He knocked out Lot and all the rest of them. One day a little Baby was born in Bethlehem. The Devil was afraid that a champion had been born and he tried to kill Him when He was a baby. But that Baby grew up and one day challenged the Devil. I believe Jesus challenged the Devil; I do not believe the Devil deliberately faced him. I believe the Son of God challenged the Devil. He went into the ring and knocked him out three times. The Devil is not champion any more. Ever since he was knocked out by the Son of God, the Son of God is Champion! You do not have to fight the Devil alone. Nobody who is a Christian is alone. Every time I have to go He says, "I am right here with you; do not be uneasy. He is afraid of Me. Resist him. In My strength resist him!"

God never told you to run from the Devil. God said, 'Flee youthful lusts.' But God did not tell you to run from the Devil. God tells you to make the Devil run from you. He says, "Resist the devil, and he will flee from you."

God Cares for His Children

I have thought about Daniel. The people said to him, "You will have to go back on God."

Daniel said, "Somehow I just don't think I can go back on God." They hid out to watch him, and when time for prayer came old Daniel did not bluster and boast. He just went and knelt with his face toward Jerusalem.

They said, "He is doing what he was told not to do. He did not take orders from the king. Get the lions hungry; we will get rough with him."

So they took old Daniel and threw him in a lion's den. Great big, shaggy, hungry lions came up and began to smell him. I can imagine that Daniel said, "Ain't you going to eat me?"

They said, "You know, we don't want any dinner today. We are really a little nauseated. We don't know what is the matter."

Daniel looked around and there was an angel. The angel said, "Daniel, wouldn't you like to take a nap?"

Daniel said, "Well, I am getting along in years. It is not

easy for me to sleep out of my own bed. I have such a good pillow. It was made especially for me."

The angel said, "I will fix you the best pillow you ever had."

Then to one of the lions he said, "Come here, big boy. Come on over here and lie down and stretch out." Then to the rest of the lions he said, "Get on over yonder in the corner. Go on over there. Get on over there in the corner and lie down!" They all went over and lay down like babies in their mothers' laps. Then I think the angel said, "Daniel, come over here and put your head on the neck of this lion and go to sleep."

I imagine Daniel looked at him and said, "Would you mind moving him around just a little—just a little?"

The angel said, "Why do you want me to do that, Daniel?"

Daniel said, "I want to sleep with my face toward Jerusalem." And he lay his head down on the neck of the shaggy lion and went to sleep. As he slept he was fanned by zephyrs from the wings of angels and kissed by spirits from the world celestial. In his dreams he read his title clear to mansions in the sky.

If you go with Jesus you may have to go to a lion's den; but, bless God, you will not be alone.

Because the Hebrew children would not go back on God they were put in a fiery furnace. Suppose somebody told you you would be put in a fiery furnace. Suppose you had that test! You talk about Judas Iscariot's selling Jesus for thirty pieces of silver—there are church members in Chicago who have sold Him for less than that; and they were not even decent enough to hang themselves after they did it!

The Hebrew children said, "We'll have to go to the fire." And they were thrown into the fire. As they were thrown in God Almighty leaned over the battlements of Heaven and blew that fire down the throats of those who threw them in. When you try to put a child of God in the fire, God will blow the fire down your own throat, too. A child of God is as dear to God as the apple of His eye. You had better not be tampering with the children of God.

The Hebrew children began to walk around in the furnace. One of them said, "This certainly is a lovely spring day, isn't it? I thought it was going to be hot today, didn't you? But it is the most beautiful spring day I have ever seen." Listen! Every furnace is a spring day when God's child walks through the fire with God!

Paul and Silas were in jail at midnight. Their feet were in stocks and their backs were lacerated. After a while Silas said, "Paul, are you asleep?"

Paul said, "No, Silas, I am not asleep."

"Paul, do you feel bad? Does your back hurt much? Is there anything I can do for you? May I rub your back a little?"

Paul said, "No, Silas; I was not thinking about that. I was thinking about the goodness of God. Wasn't it wonderful for Jesus to die for us? Isn't it wonderful to be down here in jail for Him? Silas, let's sing something."

Silas said, "All right. You raise the tune." And they sang. I do not know what they sang. It must have been some of the Psalms. I imagine that today it would have been

> In the cross of Christ I glory,
>> Towering o'er the wrecks of time
> All the light of sacred story
>> Gathers 'round its head sublime.

Or it might have been

> Am I a soldier of the cross,
>> A follower of the Lamb?
> And shall I fear to own His cause,
>> Or blush to speak His name?

But anybody can sing, even in a dungeon with feet in stocks and back lacerated, when God the Holy Ghost is there. And God the Holy Ghost is always there when the child of God is there.

Suffering for Jesus

My old father was shot through the right knee on the battle-field of Chickamauga. He was a Confederate soldier. I used to think he thought more of his crippled knee than he did of my mother or any child he had! He used to sit and talk to the soldiers who fought above the line and the soldiers who fought below the line. They would talk about their scars. I am not sorry for soldiers who get wounded. I am sorry for the boys who come home without any scars, because if every soldier enjoys his scars as my father did his, they miss a lot of fun when they do not get hit!

My father and his friends would sit and talk. One man would tell about losing a leg at one place and would get up and walk around on the old peg. Another man would shake an empty sleeve. My father could not wait to get his story in. After a while he would get up and show how the Yankees shot him. He would explain just how the bullet went through and how he wondered why it didn't cripple him for life. He would limp a little and show them how it happened.

We had a neighbor who, my father said, was the bravest soldier he ever saw in battle. He went through four years of the war and never got a scratch. I used to be so sorry for that man. All the other men would brag about getting hit and he would blush because he did not have any scars to show for the battles.

I think it would be embarrassing to go to Heaven and look at the brow of the Son of God, look at His hands when He lifted them up, get a little peek at His side; and then look all over my body and find no scars. Say! How many scars do you have because you have followed the Son of God?

When I was a boy an old country preacher told me a story. It has stayed with me. I have never forgotten it. He said that in a certain American city there was a wicked, drunken infidel man with a drunken, infidel wife. They had a sweet little girl; and they swore she should never go to church, never hear the gospel and never see a Bible. The only time she ever heard the name of Jesus was when she heard it upon the profane lips of her family and the neighbors around her.

One day she went down the street on an errand and passed a mission door. She heard singing. She listened to the song. The music in her own heart responded, and she asked what the song meant. The mission worker told her the story of Jesus, took her inside the door and got her down on her knees. She trusted Jesus.

She went home so happy. Not knowing her mother and daddy knew the story she ran into the house and said, "Oh, Daddy; the most wonderful thing has happened to me!" She told him about being saved.

The father was drunk and he whipped her. Her little dress, stained with blood, stuck to her wounded, bleeding back. That night the mother undressed her, bathed her, put a little oil on the scars and put her to bed. The next morning the little girl waked up with a fever. A doctor was called. He said she had pneumonia. He kept coming to see her, and several days later he took the mother and father to one side and told them there was no hope. They, one on either side of the bed, stood there and watched their little girl. They loved her. They were just poor, miserable sinners. The father was sober now, and the mother was sober.

The mother said, "Darling, do you want anything?"

The little girl said, "Mother, you remember the dress I had on when Daddy whipped me?"

"Yes, darling; I remember."

"Mother, h—h—has that dress been washed yet?"

The mother said, "No, darling, Mother hasn't sent the clothes out this week."

"Well, Mother, could I see that dress?"

The mother said, "Yes, I will go get it for you."

The mother went to the soiled clothes, took the little, bloody dress out and brought it in. The little girl took it in her hand and said, "Mother, may I have the scissors?"

The mother said, "Yes, darling. Mother will get you the scissors." She brought them to her. The little girl took the scissors in her hand and said, "Mother, you don't mind, do you? You don't mind if I cut out a little piece of this bloody cloth?"

The mother said, "No, darling; but what do you want with it?"

She said, "Mother, I don't understand; but I think I am dying. You know I trusted Jesus and Daddy whipped me. But I can't help loving Jesus. I don't know much about it; but, Mother, if you don't mind I'd like to take a little piece of this bloody cloth. I want to show it to Jesus and tell Jesus that while He bled for me I got to bleed a little for Him. May I, Mother?"

She clipped the little piece of bloody cloth and then died.

When I think of all He did for me and remember that I have no scars on my body I am ashamed. I have never been in jail for Him. I sometimes almost envy the martyrs that have had to die.

He is calling you Christians tonight to walk with Him. It may be that He is calling you to walk with Him through valleys, temptations, sorrows and trouble. He is calling some of you young people and some of you older ones who have wandered away from Him to come back to Him. And He is calling some of you who have never known Him to go with Him. Let's do it. What do you say?

Chapter 2

"AND PITCHED HIS TENT TOWARD SODOM"

"And Abram went up out of Egypt, he and his wife, and all that he had, and Lot with him, into the south. And Abram was very rich in cattle, in silver, and in gold. And he went on his journeys from the south even to Beth-el, unto the place where his tent had been at the beginning, between Beth-el and Hai; Unto the place of the altar, which he had made there at the first: and there Abram called on the name of the Lord. And Lot also, which went with Abram, had flocks, and herds, and tents. And the land was not able to bear them, that they might dwell together: for their substance was great, so that they could not dwell together. And there was a strife between the herdmen of Abram's cattle and the herdmen of Lot's cattle: and the Canaanite and the Perizzite dwelled then in the land. And Abram said unto Lot, Let there be no strife, I pray thee, between me and thee, and between my herdmen and thy herdmen; for we be brethren. Is not the whole land before thee? separate thyself, I pray thee, from me: if thou wilt take the left hand, then I will go the right; or if thou depart to the right hand, then I will go to the left. And Lot lifted up his eyes, and beheld all the plain of Jordan, that it was well watered every where, before the Lord destroyed Sodom and Gomorrah, even as the garden of the Lord, like the land of Egypt, as thou comest unto Zoar. Then Lot chose him all the plain of Jordan; and Lot journeyed east: and they separated themselves the one from the other. Abram dwelled in the land of Canaan, and Lot dwelled in the cities of the plain, and pitched his tent toward Sodom. But the men of Sodom were wicked and sinners before the Lord exceedingly."—Genesis 13:1–13.

*N*OW PLEASE note these two verses: "Abram dwelled in the land of Canaan, and Lot dwelled in the cities of the plain, and pitched his tent toward Sodom. But the men of Sodom were wicked and sinners before the Lord exceedingly."

This thirteenth chapter of Genesis tells the story of two men who had reached a time of crisis in their lives. It tells the story of magnanimous Abraham and selfish Lot.

Christians Ought to Get Along Without Strife

I want you to think about Abraham for just a minute. He said, "Let there be no strife, I pray thee, between me and thee, and between my herdmen and thy herdmen: for we be brethren. Is not the whole land before thee?" He really was saying, "You take what you want; I'll take what is left."

Then notice a very significant statement. "The Canaanite and the Perizzite dwelled then in the land." Abram and Lot were in that country as God's representatives. Around them, the representatives of God, there were the Canaanites and the Perizzites, the men who did not know their God.

There is nothing in all the world that hurts the cause of Jesus Christ more than strife among God's people; there is nothing more destructive. I want to stop here just a minute. I want you to get this statement; I do not want you to lose it. You are supposed to have convictions. You are supposed to believe something. If you are a Christian, you are supposed to believe the Bible is the Word of God. You are supposed to believe in the incarnation of Jesus Christ. You are supposed to believe in the vicarious blood atonement. I do not believe any man is a Christian who does not believe in the vicarious blood atonement. You may not know, when you come to Christ, what *vicarious* and *substitutionary* mean, but when any born-again man knows what those words mean, he says, "That is true. That is true!" His heart answers to the truth of the substitutional, vicarious blood atonement.

Somebody said to me, "Can a man be saved and not believe

in the deity of Christ?" Listen, I will put it this way: all saved people believe in the deity of Christ. You may not understand what deity means when you come to Jesus, but after you trust Him when somebody tells you that Jesus is God, your heart says, "That is right." And so you also, after you are saved, always believe in the vicarious atonement and the blood atonement, and you believe in the resurrection, and so on.

Now, we folks who believe these fundamental things ought to get along. Of course I am not going to swallow a lot of these big programs put on by modernistic conspirators. I refuse to give my money to support a modernistic program— missionary, educational, or any kind of program. I refuse to do it. Listen, it would be just as logical for an American to buy a German a gun with which to shoot American soldiers as it is for an orthodox Christian to support modernistic institutions and modernistic causes.

But we Christian people ought not be divided. We folks who believe the Bible, we folks who stand for something, ought to get along individually. "If it be possible, as much as lieth in you, live peaceably with all men" (Rom. 12:18).

I remember years ago when we lived in a certain city my wife and I were sitting on our front porch one morning talking. I looked across the street and saw a woman going down the street. She had her head up in the air. She bowed across the street and spoke to us, but she did not look at a woman sitting on a porch on the other side. I said to Mrs. Jones, "What is the matter?"

"Oh," she said, "They don't speak any more."

"They don't speak?"

"Oh, no. They are members of the church all right, and are supposed to be good Christians; but they don't speak any more. You know she has some chickens and the other woman has some flowers. The chickens scratched up the flowers, and they don't speak now."

Listen, men and women! I would rather have the dove of peace sing in my heart than to have all the chickens that ever scratched up anybody's flowers! And I would rather have the flowers of God's grace blooming in my soul than to have all the flowers that ever bloomed in anybody's yard. Oh, the friction! How the Holy Ghost is grieved in this country when the people of God cannot get along!

Years ago in a Georgia town I was walking down the street with a friend of mine. We passed a home and next to it was a big board wall; it must have been twenty feet high. I said to my friend, "What does that mean?"

"Oh," he said, "this family and the family next door fell out. They are mad at each other and that wall is a monument to their hatred. They put it up there to keep from seeing each other." Isn't it strange that in this world we who are children of God, we who call God our Father, we who call Jesus Christ our Saviour, we who plan to live forever in the same city, should have friction and trouble? Listen! If there is somebody you have mistreated, go ask him to forgive you. If there is somebody in your church with whom you have not made up, make up with him. Let us quit crippling the cause of Jesus Christ!

Now Abraham said, 'Let's not have any trouble. We are brethren.' Abraham was magnanimous. You cannot defeat a man like that. It is refreshing to meet big men, men who put first things first. I am not surprised that God called Abraham to begin a new race, to be the father of a nation.

Somebody said to me not long ago, "Do you believe in election?" Yes, sir, I believe in election. I will tell you the kind of election I believe in. If I wanted to build a house, I would go out in the woods and try to elect a tree that would make the best timber to serve the purpose I had in mind. I think that God always picks the best man He can find to do the job that He wants done. Say what you please about Abraham; he had his faults, but there was one thing true about him: when he was tested, most of the time he was a big man. He had enough initiative and enough determination to get up and move out under God's orders, and in an hour of crisis like this, he was magnanimous and unselfish. He said, 'Let's not have any strife. We are brethren; let's live in peace.'

Lot's Choice Put Material Things First

I imagine Lot looked around and said, "Is that so? Well, I will let you know what I want." I imagine he went home that night and talked to his wife about it. He probably said, "You know, dear, Uncle Abraham said that we could have any part of the country we want. We had some trouble. We have so many cattle that we get in each other's way, and our herdmen are having trouble. Abraham said we ought not to have any trouble, so he said that I could take whatever I want. What will we do about it?" I do not know that he spoke to his wife, but if he was like the average man, he did. It is sort of human nature for a man, when he wants to "sell out," to want to have his wife's consent. He wants somebody to agree with him. Isn't it funny how we humans are about this?

A student came into my office at the college not long ago and tried to get me to advise him to do a certain thing. He said, "I would like to do so-and-so. What do you think about it?"

I said, "Well, I don't think it is the thing to do."

He kept arguing, and finally I said, "Did you come in here to get advice, or did you come in here to convince me that you ought to do what you want to do?" It is so natural for a person to try to get somebody else to endorse the thing he is about to do, especially if the person has a question in his mind about whether it is right to do what he is about to do.

Lot, I imagine, said, "What do you think about it?"

She possibly said, "That is fine land, you know. It is well-watered land."

He may have replied, "Oh, yes, I have thought about that."

She may have answered, "We would be near town, too. I would like to live near town. You know, they say Sodom is a bad place; but they do have a White Way there." (I just imagine this—knowing women as I do.)

So Lot, I imagine, went back the next day and said, "Say, Uncle Abraham, I'll tell you what I will do. I will take this land near Sodom."

"Lot, what are you doing?"

"It is good land on which to raise cattle," he answers.

"Yes, Lot, but it is a rotten place to rear children! It is all right for your cows and your heifers and your goats and your sheep and your donkeys; but Lot, what about your children?"

Listen. Lot is not the only man who ever took better care of his cattle than he did of his children. There are women here in Chicago who protect their dogs better than they protect their babies. There are mothers in this city who, if their dog were lost and they did not know where to find it, would go and look all over town; yet they will let their daughters go to Hell and never be disturbed. There are millions of people who put sheep and horses and cows and dogs above the welfare of children. Lot was a materialist. A materialist is a man who puts the material above the spiritual.

I asked somebody the other day if a certain preacher had been called to a certain church.

"Oh yes. He gets a fine salary."

"But," I said, "he had a greater opportunity in the last place."

"Yes, he doesn't have much of a crowd now, but it is an endowed church, and he is well paid."

Listen. A preacher who goes from one place to another because he can get more money is a materialist. If money is a dominating thing in the hour of crisis, you are a materialist. A Christian has no right to choose a job simply because it pays.

I remember in the Bible a verse of Scripture, "But my God shall supply all your need according to his riches in glory by Christ Jesus" (Phil. 4:19). God has signed His name to a blank check, and put that check in the hand of every surrendered Christian on earth. He says, 'If you will go My way, I will supply your needs.' God never says, "I will give you all you want." God knows better than to promise some people that. God Almighty has not enough in this universe to give some men all they want. There are men in Chicago who if God said, "You could have all you want," would take the city, would take the state, would take the continent, the earth, the moon and the stars, and then they would walk up to God and say, "Get off your throne and let me have it." God did not say He would give you what you want. But God said, 'I will supply your needs.' No man has to sell out. There are no circumstances in life under which any man has to do wrong. Oh, the materialism in this country! A lot of us Christians pat ourselves on the back and think we are so wonderful, when the dominating, guiding thing in our lives is money.

One time in the state of Indiana when I was a young evangelist, a committee came to me from a certain city and said, "Say, Bob, we have come to ask you to hold a meeting in our city." In those days I was not in any big towns. Usually I was in small towns and small cities.

"Well," I said, "what date do you want me?"

They said, "We invited Bill Sunday two or three times, but he just doesn't seem inclined to come. So we said we would just show old Bill something. You are a young evangelist. Come to our city and hold a meeting and we will give you the biggest offering any evangelist ever got." "We will make old Bill's mouth water," one of the men said.

I said, "I am booked for Hartford City, Indiana, for that date."

"But Hartford City is a little town. They can't pay you much."

I said, "Shut up!"

Listen! A Christian is entitled to any money that God gives him as long as he travels the pathway of the will of God. But any man who makes a decision based on money sells out God. You have no right to do it! When the roll call of materialists is heard in eternity, you are going to find deacons and stewards and elders and trustees and Sunday school teachers and other Christian leaders who were dominated by the love of money. It is not money that damns people. It is the *love* of money that damns them. You can be rich and not love money, or you can be poor and love it enough to damn your soul in Hell. Materialism!

In my organization one woman came to me and said, "Dr. Bob, I have an opportunity to get a position nearer home and the position pays more money than I am now getting. What do you think about it?"

I said, "What do you think about it? Are you getting along all right financially?"

"Oh, I have everything I need, and some money in the bank."

"Well, that is more than God promised. He did not say He would give you a bank account. He said He would take care of your needs, so He has done more for you than He said He would do."

"Well," she said, "It's nearer home."

I said, "Did you ask God what He wanted you to do about it?"

You have no right to accept a job just because it is near home. There may be a reason why you should take a job near home, but not just because of that. You have no right to accept a job just because there is more money in it. You know, we are measuring people in this country not by God's gold standard, but by the world's silver standard and greenback standard. We are saying, "He gets a big salary. He is well-paid." So are jockeys at race tracks! So are Hollywood actors and actresses! I have a lot of faults. I am just as full of imperfections as any of you. But never have I accepted an invitation to preach the gospel just for what I would get out of it. If I had to die tonight, I could tell God that and never bat an eye. My mind was made up when I started out with God that the spiritual would be put first. God says, "But seek ye first the Kingdom of God" (Matt. 6:33).

That is what Lot did not do. Lot said, 'Good place for cattle . . . land well watered . . . near a city . . . all that land. . . .'

"Why, Lot?"

"Because it is good land. It is a nice place for cattle, and it is near town."

So Lot sold out that day. Oh, the men I have seen who have sold out! I have met businessmen like that. I have met politicians like that. I have met deacons and elders and trustees like that. I have seen them when they came to a crisis, and they could have been big and magnanimous but they sold out like Lot. Some of you have done it. One time there came a crisis in your home life, there came the hour when you could have done the big thing and stepped over on God's side, but you sold out to the world. You sold out! You thought you made a good deal, but you just played the fool.

Keeping Up with Sodom's People!

The curtain goes up. The scene is Sodom. There is a business office there. The man sitting at his desk looks up and says, "How are the cattle? How are the donkeys? How are the sheep getting on? Taking good care of those lambs?" There is a knock on the door, and the man at the desk says, "Come in."

A man walks in and says, "Mr. Lot, I am head of the political ring in this town. We would like to have you run for alderman."

"Oh, you've got me wrong," says Lot. "I am no politician. I am just a rancher. I do not know much about this city business."

"Huh, after all we have heard about you! Say, we need some new blood in our machine. You know, even in this bad town, some of us have a bad name and we would like to get some new blood in our organization. We would like to have you in it. And we can put you in office. We always put our men in."

Lot says, "Oh, I don't think I would be interested. But I will talk to my wife about it."

"Well," the head of the political ring says, "Good-by. I'll see you again."

Lot turns around and says, "Gentlemen, isn't that interesting? Here I am, just an old rancher, and they are trying to get me to run for alderman. Interesting, isn't it? We sure have gone up, haven't we? Say, didn't I put one over on Uncle Abraham? I made a good deal, didn't I? I got the best land, didn't I? You know, Uncle Abraham is a wonderful old fellow. He is awfully magnanimous. He offered me what I wanted, and I took it. Yes, I want to know about the sheep, and what about the cattle?"

There is another knock at the door.

"Come in!"

"Hello. Are you Mr. Lot? Well, Mr. Lot, I represent the Chamber of Commerce. I want you on our board of directors. We have heard about your successes. Say, somebody told me that you put a big deal over on your Uncle Abraham. Yeah, you got all that good land. That was a great deal you made that day."

"Well, I don't get any special credit," says Lot. "You know, Uncle Abraham is very magnanimous. He offered me what I wanted and I took it. I knew it was a good place to raise cattle and I have been very successful, of course. But I don't deserve any special credit for it. It is just good land, you know."

"Well, how about getting on the board of directors of the Chamber of Commerce?"

"Well, I don't think so. I'm just a country man. I don't know anything about this city business."

"Oh, come on, Lot; we know about you. How about it?"

"I'll tell you: I will talk to my wife, and see you later." The curtain drops.

It goes up again. A woman at the door of a lovely home on Main Street presses the button and a maid comes to the door. The lady says,

"Is Mrs. Lot at home?"

"Yes. Yes, she is."

"Well, I am Mrs. So-and-So. May I see Mrs. Lot just a moment?"

"Come right in."

She comes in. Mrs. Lot comes into the room, and the visitor says,"Mrs. Lot, I'm Mrs. So-and-So. I have a dancing school here in town and I would like to have your daughters in my class."

"Oh," Mrs. Lot says, "we never did anything like that out in the country. We are country folks, you know. My daughters never have danced."

"I know, but you must remember that you are in town now. You must keep up with the procession. When you are in Rome, you have to do as the Romans do."

Who said that? Where did that thing start? Listen! You do as most folks in Chicago do, and you will wake up in Hell! You do as most people in the world do, and your soul will be damned. God did not tell you to keep up with the age. He told you to keep step with God in the midst of your age. And every man of God who ever lived had to go across the age. Don't you think that the world is your friend. This is the world that put Jesus Christ on a cross. It is the same world that crucified your Lord. What right have you to stand in with the world that nailed the Son of God, your Saviour, to a cross? It is the same world that crucified your Lord. Do you want to make up with a world like that? Oh, the bloody hands of this world, the same world that reached down nearly two thousand years ago and picked up a hammer with one hand and a nail with the other and put that nail in the palm of the hand of your Saviour and drove it through! This world has bloody hands! When it applauds you, you can hear the blood splatter. Do you want that? Do you want the applause of a world that nailed Jesus Christ to a cross and has His blood on its hands? I do not want it! I do not expect it. I never have had it. Let me tell you something. When the godless, unregenerated,

unsaved world gets on your side, there is something wrong
with you. Don't fool yourself.

Mrs. Lot said, "Well, I don't know. I'll talk to my husband."

The curtain drops for a moment and then comes up again.
Somebody else on the porch presses the button, and the maid
says, "Yes?"

"Is Mrs. Lot at home?"

"Yes, yes. Come right in."

"Mrs. Lot, I am Mrs. So-and-So, your neighbor. We are so
glad to have you in Sodom. We have heard so much about you
and your wonderful husband, and the marvelous deal that
your husband made and your good fortune. We would like to
have you in our bridge club."

Yes, they had a bridge club in Sodom. It may not have been
your kind, but there has always been something that marked
the world, something the world does. There has always been
a well where wicked people go to draw their pleasure. There
has always been something that stamps unregenerate people.

"Why," Mrs. Lot said, "never in my life have I played a
game of cards. I don't know one card from another. You don't
know my Uncle Abraham and Aunt Sarah. They would think
we had gone to the Devil sure. But you know, I do try to
think about my children. You know, you can't be queer. I
don't know what to say, but I will talk to my husband about it
tonight."

We have a breathing spell and up goes the curtain again.
Lot is at home. He and his wife are talking. The children have
gone to bed. Lot says, "You know, dear, something very
interesting happened today. They want your husband to run
for alderman."

"Oh, they do? How wonderful!"

"Yes, and they want me on the board of directors of the
Chamber of Commerce."

"Oh, I think that is fine. That is perfectly splendid. And do
you know where they want me? They want me to join a bridge

club. The finest people in town belong to it. The banker's wife over here, and the man who owns this big plant over here —oh, yes, only the best people. I mean the best families, you know, the older families."

The older the people in Sodom were, the meaner they were. The longer they had lived there, the more momentum they got on their road to degradation. She said, "I don't know what to do. Of course, Uncle Abraham and Aunt Sarah will think we are crazy, but we have to think of the children. And you know, dear, times have changed."

Who said times have changed? Where did you get that stuff? Times have not changed!

A man said to me one time, "God Almighty has called me to preach Christian evolution. This is a new age."

I said, "In the first place, there is no such thing as Christian evolution. But even if evolution were true, it cannot do this generation any good. Even if it were so, this generation would be in Hell a million years before the universe evolved into perfection. You had better get this gang regenerated before they get to Hell."

"Times have changed." Listen! Do you want to know what times have been? All the way through, the Bible tells the story of the same human nature you have. We live under different conditions. We have automobiles. Somebody said that the automobiles have divided the race between the quick and the dead. Things are moving mighty fast.

Somebody else who was talking about the difference between this day and the old days said that in the old days a fellow would go to see his girl; they would have a fire at one end of the house and an old grandfather clock in the corner. The clock would say, "Take—your—time. Take—your— time. Take—your—time." Now a fellow goes to see his girl. The fire is in a pipe, the light is in a bottle, and the old French clock on the mantel says, "Get—together—quick! Get —together—quick! Get—together—quick!" There is only one difference between this age and all other ages: We have just

been speeding up a little. There is no difference between this
day, as far as human nature is concerned, and the days gone.
We are just traveling a little faster. A person can go to Hell
quicker. It does not take you so long to commit sin. In this
day when everything is going at high speed, it does not take
you long to commit awful sins and go to Hell. That is the
reason the penitentiaries are filled with young people. They
got a fast start to Hell.

"Times have changed. We are getting old," Mrs. Lot says.
"We must think of our children, you know. They live here.
They must go to school here, and they have to do what the
rest of them do. We can't be old-fogy all the time. Things
have broadened out anyway, and I really think we will just
have to give up a lot of that old-fogy stuff." The curtain drops.

Contrast Lot and Abraham

There is going to be a great show in Sodom. There are
wonderful times ahead of us. Let us walk out and get a little
air between the acts and refresh ourselves a little. It is a
wonderful night, isn't it? Say, let's slip down to the desert
for just a minute and see what is going on down there. We
run down there and see old Abraham and Sarah sitting at
their tent door. Abraham reaches over and gets the horny
hand of Sarah. Oh, the grandest picture in all the world is
a man and woman who have been married for years and who
are still in love, who still holds hands as they did in the old
days. Abraham and Sarah sit there in the tent door, hold
hands and look up into the sky where the stars look like
frozen dewdrops in the azure-belted dome of that oriental sky.
After a while Abraham says, "You know, dear, I am getting
a little concerned about our children. Do you remember that
letter we had from Lot the other day? He was talking about
running for alderman, and they want to get him on the board
of directors of the Chamber of Commerce. Sodom is a wicked
city; and you know, dear, there is something else, too. Lot
always was a little selfish. You remember that day when I

tried to be magnanimous and told him to take what he wanted and he chose this good land down here. Remember? I thought he was awfully selfish. I never did say anything about it." Wait a minute. Somebody has said that love is blind. Love is not blind. Love just does not always tell what it sees. When the prodigal son was over in that far-away land, I think the father many a night turned over in bed and said to the wife, "Dear, what is the matter? Are you worried?"

"No, I'm not worried. Are you?"

"No, I'm not worried. What is the matter?"

"I'm just thinking." Just thinking. Do you know what they were thinking about? They were thinking about their boy, their boy away from home. They remembered little traits in him when he was a child. They had not forgotten them; they just did not talk about them. Abraham remembered some things that he probably did not tell Sarah.

Say, but it is too dull back here in the desert. Who wants this dull desert scene? Let's go back. As we walk away we hear the lowing of cattle and the jingle of camel bells and donkey bells. We rush back to the city for the next act, and up the curtain goes.

Oh, boy, what a show! Lot has been elected alderman. He is at the gate. The crowd is saluting him. Everybody is saying, "Hurrah for Lot, the man who made good in the city! He came from the country and made a fortune. Look at Lot! Hurrah for Lot!"

Mrs. Lot is at a party playing bridge, trying to smoke her first cigarette.

You know, it is funny what folks will do for the Devil. They will get sick for him in order to learn a bad habit. Not long ago I saw a girl trying to smoke her first cigarette. I cannot get used to that thing. When I was a boy every woman on earth was as pure to me as driven snow on mountaintops. I just cannot get accustomed to these women and girls, boisterous and loud, coming out of cocktail lounges under the influence of liquor. I cannot get used to it! Somehow I cannot accustom myself to what is happening. Somehow I can understand men's being bad, but I cannot understand women and girls going to Hell. I just cannot take it in.

I remember my mother. There was not a bad woman in twenty-five miles of my boyhood home. Everybody was decent. Girls could blush. Women were modest. And there was only one divorcee in twenty-five miles of my boyhood home. Oh, the tragedy of horrors in our day!

Lot's wife is there at a party. The children are at a dance, a big ball. Everything is fine. Hurrah for Sodom, the city of excitement! The curtain is down. We walk out and say, "We will get a bit of air. My, it is exciting, isn't it? I wish I knew how it was going to come out. It must be wonderful. A thing couldn't start like this and not turn out all right. We will be back in just a minute, and see. The next act is going to be wonderful."

How Life in Sodom Turns Out

We go back and sit down. The curtain goes up, and there on the stage is a family scene. Lot is at home, talking to his wife and children. Some visitors are there. They are different from other visitors. They have tender, wonderful voices, and yet a strange dignity. Oh, wait a minute; they are heavenly guests, and they are talking.

"Yes, Lot, we have a torch of the wrath of God to burn up this town, but we were over there in the wilderness talking to your Uncle Abraham. Your Uncle Abraham said to give you a break, give you a chance. And we just thought we would come in and tell you before it happens."

Then there is a voice. There is a noise at the door and there is excitement. Lot says, "No, no, no; don't come in, gentlemen! No, no. Wait; listen, please. No. I have some guests here. Please don't." These angelic messengers go to the door. The wicked degenerates around the door are smitten with blindness. Lot goes back, and they say to him, "Go out and tell your sons-in-law and your daughters. Go tell them to get ready quickly. They haven't a chance after the fire starts, after the wrath of God is poured out. Tell them that God will not stand it any longer. Tell them that He is a God of justice, that His wrath will not hold out forever. Tell them that He is about to pour out His fire on the city. Tell them to get ready, to get out quickly while they have a chance."

Lot says, "All right. Dear, you stay here. All right, children. I will go and wake the married children." In all literature there has never been a picture as tragic as this. Shakespeare never wrote anything like it. In all the literature in all the world you cannot find anything like it.

Old Lot starts down the street. He passes muttering, cursing, perverted degenerates who say, "Yeah, what do you know about God? Hey, here's Lot! He talked about God when he came to Sodom!" Lot goes on through the crowd. The angelic messengers are protecting his family.

He comes to a home, knocks. "Children! Children! This is your father. I have sad news for you. This city is going to be destroyed. And some angelic messengers are over at my home. They have been talking to your Uncle Abraham, and Uncle Abraham prayed for us. We have a chance to get out before doom. Get up, children! Get up!" The Bible says, "But he seemed as one that mocked unto his sons-in-law."

I think I can hear them saying, "Aw, shut up! What do you know about God? Shut up!" They were probably at home drunk and arguing after a night of riot and dissipation. They said, "You don't know anything. Shut up. We're not going to leave this town. It's a wonderful place and everybody is having a good time. We aren't interested in that old-fogy stuff you used to talk about. It is all right for your Uncle Abraham and Aunt Sarah. They do not know any better. That is all right for your generation, but not for us. We have hit our stride and we are going to have our fun."

Lot goes back to his home, broken and crushed. He gathers around him his wife and two of his daughters, and they start out, out beyond the city, out beyond the danger point. He says, "Don't look back! Don't look back! Don't look back!"

His wife says, "Oh, dear, our other children, our children! Has the fire started? Will God burn them?"

"Don't look back; don't look back! If you look back, you will turn to a statue of salt. The fire from the wrath of God will kill everywhere."

There is the odor of burning flesh. What do you smell, Lot? Your donkeys are burned. Your cattle are dead. The land is dried up.

Lot says, "I am not thinking about cattle. My children! My children! My children! My wife!"

Oh, what a fool he was! And listen, there is a fool here tonight. You never saw a crowd this big promiscuously gathered without a fool in it. There is somebody here tonight who has sold God out. You cannot get away with it; God will not let you. You will smell burning flesh, too, and you will see the flash of God's anger upon your compromise. You cannot get away with it. That business just will not work. Lot took only two of his children out with him, and those who went with him disgraced his name.

I remember preaching years ago in a country community in Alabama on Saturday. It was in the days when they had Saturday services. In a little country community this service was held. A man said to me, "Will you go home with me and have dinner?" I went to his home. He lived near the edge of a little village. When we were at the home I could hear the bones of skeletons rattling around there. Something was wrong. I saw shadows over the face of the wife and mother. I saw unshed tears in his eyes. After a while he called me and I followed him out to the cow lot. There wallowing in the filth of the cow lot was a drunken fellow about nineteen or twenty years old.

The father said, "He is my boy—my boy, and I did it! I did it!"

I said, "I thought you were a Christian."

"I am a Christian, but I backslid and went into the world

for a while, went away from God at the formative period of this boy's life. I came back to God, but I had to leave my boy in sin. I got right, but I had to leave him behind me."

You cannot beat that game. Nobody ever beat it. Nobody ever will beat it. You cannot compromise and walk away from God and sell God out and get away with it. Nobody ever has. Lot lost his money. He lost some of his family. He lost the respect of his neighbors. Nobody respects you when you sell out.

You know, there is one thing you do not have to beg for and that is respect. You may have to pray for bread. You may have to plead for sympathy. You may have to beg somebody to love you, but you can command respect.

When people went out to take Jesus Christ and His eyes looked at them, they fell back. Men always salute an uncompromising character. They will respect you. They may hate you. They may curse you. They may slander you. But this dirty, Hell-bound, degenerate world still lifts it hat when uncompromising Christian people pass. You can command respect. Listen. You have lost that, some of you. Your neighbors know you, and people in churches where you go do not respect you any more. I would rather be dead—I have been cursed and slandered a good deal in my life, but the meanest enemy I ever had knows I am not for sale.

How Terrible to Lose God's Fellowship!

Oh, what Lot lost! He lost all his cattle, all his land. His children were burned. His wife was gone. He lost his honor, lost his good name. He lost his reputation. He started a stream of sin and damnation that has come across the ages. But he lost something else. Now you listen closely. He lost fellowship with God. I am not discussing with you now whether apostasy is possible or impossible. We will skip that. I am not talking about that. We will talk about what all of us agree about. Whether you believe that men can lose it or whether you believe they cannot lose it, we all agree about one thing: you can get out of fellowship with God. So we will talk about what we all agree on.

It is supposed by commentators that the angel of the covenant in the Old Testament was God. The angel of the covenant did not go to Sodom to get Lot. Three messengers went to Abraham's tent. The angel of the covenant was one of them. There were two other angels there. Those angels were the hounds of God's judgment that picked up the trail of Lot out there near Abraham's home and followed that trail to Sodom. The hounds of God's judgment always pick up the trail. The hounds of the judgment of God are on your trail tonight. You know, this scares me. I am scared! It terrifies me when I think of all the tragedies of character ruined through all the ages; when I think of men who walked with God and whose lights have gone out.

Some time ago I was in a city in a revival and a newspaper story said, "There lives in this town a man who used to be an evangelist. He held great meetings and we are remembering that meeting while Bob Jones is here. This evangelist is no longer an evangelist." I went to see him and he was an elevator boy, an old man with stooped shoulders, then an elevator boy. He was a man who had spoken to thousands. I have heard of him in all parts of America. Oh, what a tragedy! One time the road parted and he took the wrong road. Tragedy, tragedy! He got out of fellowship with God. God said, "I will pull Lot out of the fire like a brand from the burning, but I cannot keep company with him; he has sold out and I cannot fellowship with a man like that."

Years ago Dr. George Truett, then pastor of the First Baptist Church in Dallas, Texas, who to my mind was the most princely preacher in America in his day, said that years ago in his church in Dallas there was a woman, a wonderful Christian, a prominent woman. Her husband was a worldly, wicked man with a lot of money and a lot of worldly influence. He never darkened the door of a church. But his wife was a Christian. When the wife's only baby was born she was left with a leaking heart and was rarely able to come to church. When the little boy grew up to be about ten or eleven years old he was converted, and she did manage to come to church the day he joined the church and was baptized. Dr. Truett said that one day he had a phone call to come quickly over to that home. He said, "I just naturally figured that the woman was probably dying since she had heart trouble. As quickly as possible I got over. The family physician and the husband met me. I said, 'Oh, yes.'

" 'No, it is not what you think, Doctor. It is not my wife but my boy who is dying!'

" 'Oh, your boy?'

" 'Yes, my boy is dying, Doctor.'

"The physician said, 'Yes, he is dying.'

" 'Well, I am sorry, very sorry. What can I do?'

" 'Well,' the husband said, 'You know I'm not a religious man, but my wife is very devout. She prays. She is a member of your church. My little boy joined your church not long ago. His mother was very happy about it. My wife has heart trouble. And I am afraid that when the boy dies, it will kill her. I don't think she can stand it. The shock will be more than she can stand. I thought if you could come, you might bolster her up a little bit and help her.' "

Dr. Truett said he went in, sat down by the bed, took her little thin hand in his, and said, "You understand, don't you?"

"Oh," she said, "Yes, Doctor Truett. My baby is dying; I know."

"Well, you are a Christian. Your husband isn't. Neither is your physician. And they are afraid that the shock will kill you because your heart is weak. But I told them that it wouldn't, that you would stand up. I told them that God's grace would sustain you, that your Christian faith would take you through. And you must be brave."

"Oh," she said, "Don't worry about me, Doctor. I'm all right. It won't kill me. I gave that baby to Jesus before he was born. And you know, Doctor, he has been saved. You remember that Sunday I brought him down there, and he walked up and confessed Christ, and you baptized him. Oh, he is all right, Doctor Truett. I gave him to the Lord and if the Lord wants him, He can have him. Of course I'll miss him. He is a precious, wonderful baby. But don't worry about me. I'll be all right."

Dr. Truett said that all day he went from her room to the other room where the boy was dying. Late in the afternoon when the chill from the black wind of death fanned the face of the boy, the stare got in his eyes, and the jarring rattle of death in his throat, Dr. Truett looked at the physician and the physician said, "You had better go ask her if she would like to come in."

The husband, the doctor, and Dr. Truett walked in. And Dr. Truett said, "Do you want to go see your boy?"

"Yes, I want to kiss him good-by."

Dr. Truett said, "We will carry you in."

"Oh," she said, "You need not. I can walk."

She got up. Dr. Truett took one arm and her husband took the other. They walked in the room, she got down on her knees by his bed, wiped the sweat from his brow, kissed him and said, "You darling, precious baby! You have been such a sweet baby. Mother gave you to Jesus. You accepted Jesus as your Saviour, and now Jesus is going to take you Home. He is going to take you away from me, but it is all right. Jesus wants you, and whatever He wants is all right with me."

A moment later the boy slipped away, and she said, "That is all right, Jesus; You can have him. I'll be coming myself pretty soon. Thank You, Jesus, for saving him. I am so glad I am on the way, too, Jesus."

The great big athletic husband began to tremble like a leaf in the wind. He fell down on his knees beside his wife and said, "God, I won't stand it! I won't stand it! I won't give him up! I can't! I can't give him up! I won't do it!"

The little frail woman put her arm around the convulsive form of her husband and said, "Now dear, wait. Listen to me just a moment. You must not do that, dear. You must trust Jesus. Why don't you trust Him, dear, right now? Trust Him. Our baby has gone to Heaven, and I am on my way; why don't you trust Him and come and go with us? Just listen. Just be quiet. Listen to me; I want to talk to you, dear." And she opened up the Word to him.

Dr. Truett said, "I stood there and watched that little woman, who they thought would die from the shock, talk to her husband, that great big athletic man, and try to get him quiet, and I said, 'There is no substitute in human life for the presence of God.' " Oh, it is wonderful!

Oh, listen a moment. The Devil does not have anything for you. Men and women, the Devil does not have anything! The Devil never produced an oak. The Devil never painted a flower. The Devil never lighted a star. The Devil never put any gold and silver in the mines. The Devil never made the flowers to grow. The Devil does not own anything. All he has is stolen property. And if you take something from him and turn your back on God, you are taking stolen property. You cannot get away with it. Let's come clean with God. Let us do it tonight!

Chapter 3

OPPORTUNITY ON WHEELS

"And the angel of the Lord spake unto Philip, saying, Arise, and go toward the south unto the way that goeth down from Jerusalem unto Gaza, which is desert. And he arose and went: and, behold, a man of Ethiopia, an eunuch of great authority under Candace queen of the Ethiopians, who had the charge of all her treasure, and had come to Jerusalem for to worship, Was returning, and sitting in his chariot read Esaias the prophet. Then the Spirit said unto Philip, Go near, and join thyself to this chariot. And Philip ran thither to him, and heard him read the prophet Esaias, and said, Understandest thou what thou readest? And he said, How can I except some man should guide me? And he desired Philip that he would come up and sit with him. The place of the scripture which he read was this, He was led as a sheep to the slaughter; and like a lamb dumb before his shearer, so opened he not his mouth: In his humiliation his judgment was taken away: and who shall declare his generation? for his life is taken from the earth. And the eunuch answered Philip, and said, I pray thee, of whom speaketh the prophet this? of himself, or of some other man? Then Philip opened his mouth, and began at the same scripture, and preached unto him Jesus."
—Acts 8:26-35.

*T*HIS IS the special verse to which I wish to call attention: "Then Philip opened his mouth, and began at the same scripture, and preached unto him Jesus."

Tonight I want to talk to you about a kind of work that every Christian in the wide world can do, one kind of job you can do for God. Do not try to excuse yourself. Do not say it is not your business, not your work. Every Christian can do this job, the job of personal work.

I am taking it for granted that most of you are Christians; and if you are, it is your business to go out from this service, find sinners, tell them what to do to be saved and then try to get them to do it.

If as you go home tonight you should find a man underneath a wrecked automobile and he should turn his dying, staring eyes up into your face and say, "Look here, friend; I am dying. I will be here just a minute. I am going out into eternity. Can you tell me what to do to be saved?" I wonder if you could. I would be ashamed to call myself a Christian if I were not able to tell people what to do to be saved. There are some things in the Bible I do not understand— things too deep, too high, and too broad for me. There are things that I have never grasped, depths which I have never explored. But there is one thing in the Bible as clear as the light of the clearest noonday, and that is the plan of salvation. "By grace are ye saved through faith; and that not of yourselves: it is the gift of God. Not of works, lest any man should boast" (Eph. 2:8,9). Any Christian in five minutes' time can sit down and learn what to say to a lost man and tell him how to be saved. You do not have to be a theologian. You do not have to go to school or college. Any ordinary man can go out and tell the lost what to do to be saved.

One morning at our college chapel I said, "Now, boys and girls, [that is what I call my students. Of course it is not very collegiate. I should say, 'young ladies and young gentlemen,' but I say, 'boys and girls.'] get your pencils and paper. I am going to suppose that a man is dying. He will be dead in five minutes. He is on his way to Hell and you are the only person in the world who can tell him what to do to be saved. I will give a Bible to the student in this college who will write the best statement in your own words that you would give to such a man. I want every one of you students to be an expert at this business of winning souls."

The papers came in. We sent them through the Bible Department and through the Department of English. A little

Episcopalian girl who had just come to college, a girl who had been saved only a short while, wrote the most remarkable statement. I do not remember just what she said, but it was about the clearest statement I ever read in print by a theologian or anybody else on what to do to be saved.

The trouble with most of us who call ourselves Christians is that we have never really surrendered to God. Honestly now, have you ever done it? Are you out-and-out for God? The trouble with most of us is that we just have not come clean with God. In a way we have given God our hearts and we are trying to trust Him. We hope that when we die we will go to Heaven. Some of you folks have just enough religion to keep you uncomfortable. You are always afraid the Devil is going to get you. You would not want to die suddenly for anything in the world. You are hoping that when you go to die you will be conscious and have plenty of time so that if you do not have things fixed, you can fix them. Most of you are going through the world with just enough of Jesus to keep you from enjoying the world and just enough of the world to keep you from enjoying Jesus. A little bit of religion is a very uncomfortable thing.

I remember an old-time country doctor that I saw down South, one of those old quinine-and-calomel doctors, the kind that gave people quinine externally, internally and eternally! I saw him take a big dose of calomel on a knife, put it on a man's tongue and say, "Swallow it."

I looked at him and said, "Doctor, it is none of my business, but aren't you afraid you'll give that fellow too much of that stuff?"

He said, "No, no; a little calomel will just upset him. A big dose will not make him sick."

"Well," I said, "Doctor, I didn't know that was so about calomel but I know it is so about the religion of Jesus Christ." A little dose of it keeps you always nauseated and upset. But, brother, when you come clean with God, when you come out-and-out for God, it makes all the difference in the world.

God Wants Your Body: Your Hands, Feet, Tongue

Now, let me ask you something: have you ever surrendered to God? Have you ever given God your hands? How many times have you ever lifted your hands when you did not have back of the effort a selfish purpose? Have you ever given God your feet? Wait a minute; don't you dodge tonight! Don't you use your feet just to walk around and attend to your own business? What about your eyes? Did you ever give your eyes to God? Don't you use your eyes to see just the things you want to see, the things that delight you and entertain you? Did you ever walk up and say, "God, I want to give You my ears. They are filled with so many sounds, so many words, and so many voices. God, I want to give You my ears. I want You to un-stop them so I can hear the cry of the heart that needs God." Have you ever given God your tongue? Oh, these long, mean tongues some of us have! Sam Jones said he knew a woman down South who had a tongue so long she could sit in the parlor and lick the skillet in the kitchen. These long, slan-derous tongues some of us have! We are always talking and saying things. Say, did you ever give your tongue to God? God wants your tongue. God has something He wants you to tell people.

Have you ever surrendered to God? People talk about giv-ing God their hearts. When you came to Jesus you did not give God anything. When you came to Jesus you came not to give Him your heart but to get a new heart, a heart from sin set free. Now that you are saved God wants you to give Him something. You could not give God anything when you were a sinner. You had nothing to give God but your sins which Jesus Christ bore in His body on the cross. But after you got saved, then you had something God wanted. He still wants it. I will tell you what it is: it is your body.

Around Christmas time in our home we begin to talk about what we want for Christmas. I say to Mrs. Jones, "Do you know what Bob would like to have? Do you know what Fanny

Mae [that is Bob's wife] would like to have? Do you know what Bobby III would like to have? What would your mother like to have?" We begin to try to find out what they want so we can get those things. You see, we love each other.

God does not hint to you. Listen! The Lord Jesus Christ stands here tonight—oh, if we only had eyes to see Him! He stands here on this platform. He is right there by you. He is looking into your face and saying, "I saved you one time. I would like for you to do something for Me. You have something I want you to give Me. You have something I really want." Listen! How can you resist Jesus Christ? He says, "Here is My brow. I gave that brow for a crown of thorns. I did it for you. And here is My back; look at it. That is what I did for you. These hands of Mine—look at them. I did it all for you. Now there is something I would like to have you do for Me. I want you to give Me something. I want your body." Listen, your body is your contact with earth. God wants some feet around Chicago to run errands of mercy. God wants some ears in this city to hear the cry of thousands of hearts that are crying for God even when they do not know why they cry. God wants human eyes to see lost men and human tongues to tell these men the story of redeeming grace.

The Old Testament tells the story of a dead child. Somebody said, 'We had better send for the preacher.' That is the only time some people send for the preacher—when somebody dies, or sorrow comes, or skeletons break out of closets. So they said, 'Go tell the prophet. GO TELL THE PROPHET!' Word was sent to him.

The prophet was busy. He said, 'Here is my rod. Take it and put it on the child.'

After a while they came back and said, 'Say, preacher. The rod is no good. We laid the rod on the child, but he is still dead.'

The old prophet said, 'I suppose I had better go myself.' He went over there, laid his body down on the body of the child and the child came to life. Listen! God wants your body.

He is asking for it tonight. Oh, men and women, if this crowd should ever surrender to God!

You remember that passage of Scripture which says, "I beseech you therefore, brethren, by the mercies of God, that ye present your bodies a living sacrifice, holy, acceptable unto God, which is your reasonable service" (Rom. 12:1). That passage of Scripture is addressed to Christians. We know from the word *brethren* that the writer is talking to Christians. He is saying, 'I beseech you Christians to give God your bodies.' What are you going to do about it? Are you going to turn Him down? Are you going to say no to Him? Or are you going to walk up and say, "Lord, I'm so sorry I have been so mean and selfish, but I will give You my hands. They are not much good, but You may have them. God, if they are any good to You, You may have them. And, God, here are my feet. I've been running on errands of sin, but now I give You my feet. I am going to start out to run errands of mercy. And my eyes, You may have them, too. [Oh, these eyes have led so many of us astray!] You can have my eyes, God, and my tongue, and my ears—everything else I have." Let's come clean with God! Let's quit all this shamming business! Listen! Let's quit this humbuggery stuff in this country! Let's surrender our lives to God and come out and out for the Lord Jesus Christ. What do you say?

God Wants Your Level Best

The average Christian in this town is not doing as much to win souls to Jesus Christ as the average politician is doing to win votes. If you Christians went after sinners like politicians go after votes, you would get souls like politicians get votes. The politicians of this town have the town divided. The political bosses know all the people and who they are kin to. They are organized. They know their job. Here is a man running for office. He goes out to see a certain man. The man is not at home, but he goes back the next day, and keeps on until he sees him. After a while he says, "Bill, I am running for office.

I want you to vote for me. We are old buddies, you know. We have been in the same crowd. And, Bill, how about your mother and father and your grandparents? You have a lot of kinfolks, Bill." Did you ever do that much to keep sinners from going to Hell? We say that we love Jesus; we are orthodox. We believe all the Bible. Yes, sir, we are fundamentalists. We believe the Bible from cover to cover. You can't put us with that modernistic crowd—not us! Well, we do not act like it. We have loved ones and friends who have between them and Hell just a little heartbeat and we do not seem so much concerned.

A man said to me not long ago, "Heaven is far away and Hell seems like a distant land." Why, you Christians do not know how close you are to Heaven! There is just a heartbeat between you and that place. And listen, sinner: if you are sitting back there without God tonight, the only thing between you and Hell is that pump, pump of your heart that may stop any minute. I would hate to think that the only thing between me and Hell was a heartbeat. I bless God that between me and Hell is a cross and on that cross a bleeding Lamb.

You have loved ones and some of your best friends—people who are dear to you—and the only reason they are not in Hell is that their hearts are still beating. And people are dying with heart trouble by the thousands today. Did you know that you are playing at this soul winning job? We are supposed to have 225 churches in this campaign. If this were a Devil's show people would be hanging from the rafters. Let us say that there are a hundred church members in each of these churches. There are more than that. There are many hundreds of them. There are multiplied thousands of them who believe that God can save men from Hell and take them to Heaven. There are thousands of us orthodox Christian people in Chicago. God, help us to wake up and get busy! We have the greatest business on God Almighty's earth. I am ashamed of us! God be merciful to us poor, lazy, good-for-nothing

Christians! The last one of us ought to be on our faces before God, begging Him to have mercy on our poor souls. How indifferent we are! How unconcerned we are!

There is a story of an old preacher who walked up to a lady on the mezzanine floor of a hotel and said, "Lady, lady! Are you saved?"

She began to cry. He quoted a verse of Scripture and walked on. A few moments later her husband came and found her crying. He said, "What is the matter with you?"

"Oh," she said, "Dear, the strangest man you ever saw walked up here a few minutes ago and asked me if I were saved."

"Why didn't you tell him to attend to his own business?"

"Oh," she said, "But dear, if you had seen him you would have thought he was attending to his own business."

Listen! That *is* your business. Your business is to witness to the saving power of Jesus Christ wherever you go. Do you know what your vocation is? Your vocation is your main business in life. Your avocation is a side line. Your vocation is the job of winning souls. Keeping house or filling a job is not your vocation. That is your avocation. Witnessing for Christ is your vocation. May God move on our hearts. May He stir us to our depths! I have been searching my own heart lately. I am ashamed of myself. I am preaching to all of us preachers. We preachers ought to be ashamed of ourselves. You deacons and stewards and elders, you Christian leaders, ought to be on your faces before God, begging Him to forgive you for your laziness and for being no-account. You are neglecting your job. If any business in this town had an employee who did not stick to his job any better than you Christians stick to yours, that employer would fire the employee. We go on with a good God and neglect it. Aren't you ashamed of yourself? I am ashamed of myself. We ought to be.

A man said to me, "Bob Jones, you are killing yourself." Don't tell me that! What is a better way to die than this? Men are wearing themselves out in sin and pleasure and sensuality. Yet you and I are sitting down loafing on God's job—and patting ourselves on the back and throwing kisses at ourselves and thinking we are wonderful! The last one of us in this house ought to be weeping and begging God to pardon us and forgive us for being no good.

In the Bible we read about a big religious gathering. Suppose we call it a Bible conference. It was not really that, but that is what we will call it. There was a big convention in Jerusalem. The people were having a big time. Jesus was in town, and He went out to a pool where the angel troubled the water once a year. A man was there who had been a cripple for many years. Whoever got in the pool first after it was troubled always got well. Jesus looked at the man and said to him, 'Why don't you get in the pool when it is troubled?'

'I have nobody to help me.'

'Where are they?'

'They are over there teaching Sunday school classes.'

'Where are they?'

'They are going down the street with a Bible under their arm to hear Dr. So-and-So talk about the Antichrist.'

'Where are they?'

'They are going around trying to learn the technique of running a church.'

Can't you see them, with a songbook under one arm and a Bible under the other—going up to the temple for a great convention. And this poor cripple is out there just waiting for somebody to help him. He wants to get in. He sees the water troubled, turns his eyes that way and cannot get in because there is nobody to help him. Listen, there are sinners in Chicago going to Hell by the thousands because they have nobody to help them. Don't blame the sinners. Multiplied thousands of them would come to God if we were on the job. You say, "O Bob Jones, we have the preachers, and we supposed. . ." Wait a minute. Shut up. Shut up! You cannot get out of it like that. A preacher cannot do your job.

A man said to me not long ago, "Bob Jones, you are doing

the work of four or five men. You write for newspapers. You edit a paper of your own. You have all these many radio stations. You have much of the burden of Bob Jones College. You do as much preaching as any other evangelist in the country. You are carrying this heavy load of so many organizations. You are doing the work of four or five men!"

I said, "Don't tell me that. No man ever did the work of more than one man. My work is my dead level best." Your work is your dead level best. You cannot do my job and I cannot do yours. If you do not do your God-assigned task, throughout eternity there will be a job that has never been done. One day it dawned on me that God may have given me a key that would unlock the door of some heart and that I was the only man who had the key. O God, if that is so, please help me to unlock the door! There may be in Chicago some poor sinner that my special, peculiar style will reach and that nobody else on earth can reach. John Rice might get somebody else and Paul Rood somebody else and you somebody else. But we all have a job to do. Jesus said, "Go ye, therefore, and teach all nations. . ." No man can go into all the world. But there are enough Christians on earth that if every man would go as far as he could, we could go into all the world and preach the gospel to every creature.

Someone Will Go to Hell If You Do Not Win Him

Years ago when I was a young preacher I was holding a meeting in a little town in Louisiana. One day the pastor of a church said, "Bob, I have a funeral to conduct and I must be out of town. Will you go up to the cemetery at ten o'clock and conduct the funeral?"

I said, "Well, I do not know anything about the man."

The pastor said, "Oh, well, he is an old Mississippi swamper who died. He was an old sinner and blasphemer who never entered the door of a church. You cannot say anything for him anyhow. The family just wanted some preacher. You can read some Scripture and pray and that is all you can do."

I went to the cemetery. The coffin was brought in. There were scarcely enough people to bury him decently. He was an old miser. Nobody cares when a miser dies. Even other sinners do not care when an old miserable, miserly sinner like that dies. As I remember it, there was only one woman at the cemetery. She lived in a home nearby. She had a woman's heart in her bosom. She possibly said to herself, "They are burying something; it must be a human being." So she ran out in the yard and gathered some flowers. That was the only floral offering at the grave.

I read the Bible and prayed the best I could. We covered him up with dirt; put him to bed with a shovel. I walked out of the gate of the cemetery and stood there for a moment. I put my arm around his only living son and said, "My friend, my father died one time and my heart almost broke. I do not know what I would have done without Jesus. I want to ask you if you will not trust Jesus as your Saviour."

He looked at me for a moment. His face will haunt me in eternity. His lips quivered. The muscles of his face twitched and tears started down his cheek as he began to sob. He said, "Mr. Jones, I am thirty years old. I have lived in this community all my life and this is the first time anybody ever took any interest in my soul."

Listen! There are people in your block who will be dead before long and they will tell God that nobody in Chicago ever asked them to accept Jesus. Listen! You could evangelize your block in one day. This city of Chicago could be evangelized, if we were organized, in a week's time. The gospel could be given to practically every home in this city in a week if we were organized. I experimented down South in a rural district one time. I believe we got the gospel to ninety-nine people out of a hundred within a fifty mile area in six months. You could do the job. The trouble is we just do not do it.

Don't you want to be a soul winner? The greatest business in the world is winning souls.

You will give a doctor everything you have to operate on

your daughter and save her from death. I saw today in the newspaper the picture of that sad-faced father holding his baby, a blue baby. What you would not do to save your baby! But listen to me, the greatest business in the world is not keeping people out of jail and keeping them out of the grave. The biggest business on earth is keeping people out of Hell and taking them to Heaven. Don't you want to be a soul winner? You can be. Every Christian here can be.

If You Are Willing for God to Tell You What to Do, You Will Win Souls

The Scripture that I read to you tonight tells us that the angel of the Lord said, 'Philip, go down that road.' And he went. He did not stop to argue. He did not talk back to God. He did not say, "Now Lord, I want to ask You some questions. You are not going to call on me to pray in public, are You? I can't do that. You are not going to ask me to do personal work. That is out of my line." Don't you talk back to God. You are to be a witness. You are to go into all the world and preach the gospel, and Jesus says He will be with you. Don't you talk back to God. You can do anything God tells you to do. Back of God's commands He puts omnipotence. You can sail any sea, climb any mountain, scale any wall when God tells you to do it. I tell my students in the college never to ask where the road leads—just ask, "Am I on the right road?" The right road leads out at the right place. If you will go God's way, you will always make right contacts.

We hear talk about sanctification in this country. Don't be afraid of that word. It is strange how scared some people get. I am not talking just about fuss and emotion. There used to be a steamboat on the Tennessee River that could not blow and run at the same time. When it would blow it would have to stop running. When it ran it did not have enough steam to blow. I know some folks who cannot do anything but shout. That is all the steam they have. But, brother, if the shouting does not interfere with your engine running, shout! I am not talking about something that sounds peculiar. Don't be afraid of God's word *santification*. Someone has said, "Santification is a supreme desire not to want to have your own way." Let me say that again: "Santification is a supreme desire not to want to have your own way." How is it with you? Do you want God's way or your way?

Years ago out in Colorado one Saturday night, I dropped into a tent meeting. I was a young preacher, had led many people to Christ and had a little reputation as an evangelist. But I was an awfully stubborn, determined fellow. Seth Rees, whose son is now up here in Minneapolis, was preaching. I did not know who he was, had never seen him before. I heard his text and I heard his sermon, and I have never forgotten it. His text was: "If God be for us who can be against us." He said, "We will put it this way: 'Since God is for us, who can be against us.'" It stuck to me. He talked about men wanting their way. At the close of the service I as a young preacher walked up and knelt at that front seat, took the reins of my life out of my hands and put them into the hands of Almighty God. I told God He could have His way with me. I have not been all I ought to have been since that time. I have been blundering along the road, but I am standing here tonight saying, "God, whatever You want, that is what I want. Your way is my way."

At a recent meeting of our board of trustees of our college I said, "Ladies and gentlemen, if Jesus Christ walked in here and told us what to do, we would do it." That is what I call consecration. "Thy will, O God, in my life—not my will."

God Opens the Doors, Gives the Results for the Obedient Soul Winner

'Go down that road,' the angel said to the eunuch.

'All right,' the eunuch answered, 'I'm going.' He went down the road under divine direction. It is wonderful to march under God's orders. It is wonderful to be going the way

God said to go. You cannot miss the right road if you are out winning souls. That is God's way!

He went down there and found a man reading the Bible. That is just like God. When God sends somebody out on a job, God gets there first and fixes conditions so the job can be done. I have never had a campaign manager to get me evangelistic campaigns. All my life I have had all I could do. Never has there been a time when I did not have more invitations than I could accept. I have never hunted meetings, but have tried to follow the policy that when I have a job never to think of the next one. Do that one. I tell our students, "When you get into a room, clean up that room where God put you. Don't ask any questions. Just fix the room. When you get that room all fixed, God will open the door and put you into another one. When you get in that room, fix it all up: dust it, clean it, straighten it up. Don't leave any of it undone. When you get that job done, God may move you into a bigger room. This time you may be a little proud and stuck up—you have a big room to work in. If you get stuck up, God may put you in a little attic. If He does, go on and get in there; that is where you belong." Day after day during my life I have been going from one room to another. Some day, if the Lord tarries, I am going to be in a room somewhere. I am going to try to be busy, doing the job. After while it will get a little dark. Something is the matter with the electricity, or maybe my eyes are not good. Things are not exactly right. Oh, the lights are going out, but yonder is a door. No, it is not a door—it is not like any other door. It is a gate—a gate of pearl. It is opening, it is opening! And I am going to move into a room He fixed *for me*. Heaven must be a wonderful place. If God can turn a sunbeam into a pencil and paint a rose in one springtime, what will Heaven be? Jesus has been there two thousand years doing interior decorating. My room is all ready there. All He has been doing is touching up the inside of it.

Say, let's go with God down that road. Philip got down

there and found the eunuch reading the Bible. Listen, I testify to you Christians that under God's orders you always get results. A man said to me not long ago, "There are invisible results." Some men are good authorities on that kind of results. I know there are invisible results, but, brother, I want to see something. There are things I cannot see, but God lets us see some things. That is the glory of it.

God Uses Eager, Ardent, Enthusiastic Service

When Philip saw him reading the Bible, he "ran thither to him." I believe he literally ran. I have never known God to use a lazy man. I have known God to use crippled people, blind people, weak people, sick people. And I have known God to use people who did not have much sense. But I have never known God Almighty to use a lazy man. Study history. The men whom God has used through the ages have been men who got up and hustled. 'The king's business demands haste.'

He "ran thither to him." If you had seen him after that chariot you would have thought he was crazy. A person cannot get a dose of real, old-time religion without some people thinking he is crazy. The trouble is that we have been subnormal so long we have forgotten that Pentecost is normal Christianity. We have been running subnormal in this country. If a baby is a good baby somebody will say, "His parents will never raise that baby, he is too good." When he grows up and gets into sin and goes to the Devil like most people expected him to do, then you bring him to God and he gets on fire for God, they will say, "He is a little bit off balance. He is a fanatic."

When I was a young preacher I used to hold meetings in certain towns, little places. People would write me up in the church paper as "Rev. Robert Jones"—not "Bob Jones." They would say, "Rev. Robert Jones held a meeting in our town for two weeks and did no harm to anybody." Listen, brother, I would rather step on somebody's toes and knock

somebody out of the way on the road of life and go places for
God than to sit down and do nothing! The trains that travel
fast stir up dust but they carry the most passengers.

He ran to him. He did not go after that chariot like you go
to prayer meeting. Did you ever notice how people go to
prayer meeting on Wednesday night? Two or three will come
in. Then an old man and an old woman will come in. After
while an old fellow comes in, and the pastor says to himself,
"Well, we will start; he is always the last one." Then he gets
up and says, "I wonder if we have anybody to play the piano
tonight. Can somebody play for us? Oh, yes, there is Mrs.
So-and-So. You come and play for us. Oh, yes, come on.
Please. We are going to sing just old songs. Come on." He
pleads with her. Eventually she gets to the piano. Then she
slowly sits down and opens the songbook. That is the way
most people run God's business. You never saw a theater run
like that. The Devil's business doesn't drag like that.

After she gets fixed at last the pastor says, "We will sing,

> Blest be the tie that binds
> Our hearts in Christian love.
> The fellowship of kindred minds
> Is like to that above."

I hope Heaven is not that dull!

The Devil looks in and says, "It is the same old crowd they
had last Wednesday night. No, they are short one. Old Man
So-and-So died this week." He goes on to the picture show
and finds it packed and crowded and still others standing in
line willing to pay to get in. We ought to be ashamed of ourselves. We ought to run to our houses of worship with joy and
thanksgiving.

Soul-Winning Opportunities Pass Away Soon

Philip ran. Here was an opportunity on wheels. The opportunities of life are on wheels today. A few years ago, about
a quarter of a century ago, not far from this spot, old Bill

Sunday spoke to his thousands. His dust is sleeping out yonder in the cemetery. I want to go to his grave while I am in Chicago. He is sleeping the sleep of death. Men and women who came down the aisle and shook hands with him and came to God—many of them—are up in Heaven with him. It has not been many years since Dwight L. Moody shook this city. And Chapman moved it and other men moved it. They are dead and gone. Now you are in the first great city-wide, united campaign of this kind for a quarter of a century. What a golden opportunity to touch a city for God! The chariot is passing. Such a chariot may not pass again for another quarter of a century. Personally, I never went to a city with any heavier sense of responsibility. I came here more fatigued than I have been in many years. The most terrific strain I have had in a long time, I have had in recent weeks. But I asked God to give me strength to do my job the two weeks I am here. I do not want anybody's blood in Chicago on my hands. If this campaign does not stamp this city for God, I do not want to have to answer at the judgment seat of Christ.

You have a loved one unsaved. You could get that loved one to this meeting and get him saved. You have a friend. If you would get that friend here, he would likely be saved. I never saw such a percentage of unsaved people saved as we have had here for the last three nights. Nearly every person who comes in here unsaved, finds Christ. You never saw anything like Sunday night's service for the percentage of unsaved people. Last night it was practically a Christian crowd. You could bring the sinners in if you would, and they would come to God. The chariot is passing!

One time in my old home city, Montgomery, Alabama, I went down to a jeweler to have my watch fixed. I went back the next day to get it. A stranger handed it to me. He saw my name on the outside. "Oh," he said, "you are Bob Jones, the evangelist."

I said, "Yes."

He said, "My name is So-and-So. I have just come to the city—just started to work today."

"Well," I said, "I am glad to see you. I hope you will like our town." I stood there and talked to him for a few minutes. Then I started off. I said, "I wonder why that man wanted to meet me? Some folks run from preachers. I wonder if he is a Christian. I believe I will go back and ask him." But then I said, "No, I am busy today; I will not bother. I will see him some other time." I went on down the street but as I did, I said, "I ought to go back and talk to that man." But then I felt again, "Well, I am awfully busy today. I will make a little note and when I come downtown in the morning I will drop in to see him. I will ask him if he is saved. If he is not saved, I will try to lead him to Christ." I made a little note, put it in my pocket and went on about my business.

The next morning I got on a streetcar near where we lived and started downtown. I unwrapped my morning paper and on the first page in big headlines I saw where that man that night standing at his desk fell dead. I got downtown as quickly as possible. I rushed in and said to the proprietor who was an officer in the church, "Was Mr. So-and-So who fell dead here last night a Christian?"

He said, "I do not know. He was a stranger in town, just started to work here yesterday morning. I do not know anything about him." I do not know either. I touched that life for a moment, never to touch it again.

Life's opportunities are on wheels. You touched somebody today you will never see again this side of eternity. You sat by somebody on the streetcar; you talked to somebody in a store or shop or factory. You had a chance. You met a fellow-pilgrim on his way to eternity. The chariot passed, and that chariot will never come back to you. O God, forgive us. Forgive us Christians, God.

Are you a sinner tonight? Are you in this service unsaved? If you are, a chariot is passing tonight. It may never come back any more. Today is the day of salvation. Now is the accepted time. Do not let this chariot pass. Get in it. Join yourself to it. Trust Christ. It might be the last chariot that will ever pass.

PRAYER: Blessed Jesus, I feel guilty. This never has been easy for me, Jesus. I don't mind preaching, but it has never been easy for me to do this personal work business. It has always been the hardest thing in the world for me. I do not know whether it was my rearing or what it was, but it has never been easy. I haven't been as faithful as I should have been, and I am sorry. I want You to please forgive me, Jesus; won't You? I do love You. I want to do Your will. All of us Christians love You. The trouble is that we have just been careless. We have been taking You for granted, like we sometimes take our wives for granted or our husbands for granted. Some of us have taken mother and dad for granted, and our friends too. And we have taken You for granted. We haven't been faithful. We are so sorry. Help us to try to say a word for You on our way home tonight. We may contact somebody tonight who needs Christ and whom we could reach. Help us to do it! Amen.

Chapter 4

CHRIST'S SECOND COMING

"For Christ is not entered into the holy places made with hands, which are the figures of the true; but into heaven itself, now to appear in the presence of God for us: Nor yet that he should offer himself often, as the high priest entereth into the holy place every year with blood of others; For then (that is, if He had done that) must he often have suffered since the foundation of the world: but now once in the end of the world (the end of the age) hath he appeared to put away sin by the sacrifice of himself. And as it is appointed unto men once to die, but after this the judgment (It does not say that it is appointed unto ALL men once to die): So Christ was once offered to bear the sins of many; and unto them that look for him shall he appear the second time without sin unto salvation."—Heb. 9:24–28.

I WANT TO TALK to you about these verses. In them you have three wonderful statements: first, Christ has appeared; second, Christ does appear; third, Christ is going to appear. In these verses you have Christ appearing on the cross, Christ appearing in Heaven, and Christ appearing again to earth in glory. In these verses you have Christ dying on the cross, bearing our sins. You have Christ up in Heaven interceding for us. You have Christ coming back again to receive us. In these verses you have Christ who has been here, Christ who has gone away, and Christ who is coming back. Get it clear: He was here one time. He went away one time. He is coming back sometime. That is what these verses say.

I want you to get this clear tonight: just as certain as He was here, just as certain as He went away, just that certain He is coming back sometime.

Now wait just a minute: the Devil hates those three things.

The Devil hates the atonement. Listen, you hear people in this day and time say, "The Sermon on the Mount is my religion." Brother, the Sermon on the Mount cannot save you. It is the Preacher who preached that sermon who can save you. People talk about living up to the Sermon on the Mount. You cannot live up to the Sermon on the Mount unless you go to the cross of Calvary and get your sins washed away in the blood and get a new heart. It is not Christ preaching on the mountain, it is Christ dying on the cross to which the Bible gives special emphasis. All through the Bible the emphasis is on the cross, the cross, the cross. Christ died for us. Christ bore our sins in His body on the tree. Christ was wounded for our transgressions. He was bruised for our iniquities. Such truths are found all through the Bible. Do not forget this. Modernism puts the emphasis on the Sermon on the Mount, but the Bible puts the emphasis on Christ's dying on the cross. There are religious systems in this country that attempt to do away with the blood of Christ. I do not wish to enter into any controversial discussion tonight. I know some nice people do not agree with me about this; take, for instance, our Christian Science friends. Mrs. Eddy has a chapter in one of her books on the atonement, but it is a meaningless chapter from the conservative orthodox Christian standpoint. What becomes of the atonement if Jesus bore our sins, which were not sins, in a body, which was not a body, on a cross, which was not a cross? According to Christian Science, sin is not a fact, it is not a reality. If there is no such thing as sin, then Jesus Christ had no sin to bear in His body on the cross. If there is nothing material, He had no body with which to bear my sin. If there is nothing material, there is no such thing as a real cross on which He died. All down through the years the Devil has tried to take people's eyes off Calvary.

> I saw One hanging on a tree,
>   In agony and blood,
> He fixed His languid eyes on me
>   As near His cross I stood.

> At the cross, at the cross
>   Where I first saw the light,
> And the burden of my heart
>   rolled away.

It is to Calvary that we go. "Life begins at Calvary," as we have been singing in this campaign. The Devil does not want you to see this.

So Christ was here. He was born of a virgin. That is wonderful. He was a little babe in a manger. That is wonderful. But, bless God, the glorious thing to me is that the baby who was virgin-born and was in a manger, one day hung on a cross and died for me. He died for me! Somebody has said that that is all the gems of all people in one diadem. He died for me! That is all the flowers of all springtimes in one bouquet. He died for me! That is all daydawns of all mornings breaking forth into a glorious spring day. He died for you. Do not forget that!

Now take Christ as our intercessor. He is up at the right hand of the Father saying a good word for us. You do not need anybody else to intercede for you. You do not need a bishop or a priest or a preacher. The humblest Christian in this house has as much access to God the Father through Jesus Christ His Son as has a bishop or a priest or the Virgin Mary or anybody on this earth or in Heaven. We are a kingdom of priests, blessed be God! And we Christians under the blood can walk up to God in the name of Jesus Christ and do our own talking. Oh, how the Devil wants to veil Jesus so we will not see Him up yonder interceding for us!

Now take the second coming of Christ. Oh, how the Devil tries to discredit this glorious doctrine! In the first place, the Devil hitches all the fanatics up with this doctrine. Strange, weird people, good people, some of them, but peculiarly fanatical people, go around talking about the Lord's coming. Don't forget that He is coming again. Never mind what anybody says about it; He is really coming again. Do you know that the Devil tries to laugh out of court every doctrine in the Bible? He wants to discredit these glorious doctrines. He wants to get preachers where they will not say anything about them. Take the doctrine of holiness. Why, there is a Bible doctrine of holiness, but some people are afraid to mention the word *holiness*. They are afraid to mention the word *sanctification*. They are afraid of those words because those words have been discredited by certain extremists and a certain radical type of people. But do not mind; your business is to go right on and not hesitate to tell people that we ought to live victorious, sanctified Christian lives; that we ought to be set apart for His service.

Now take the Lord's second coming. I only heard one sermon on the second coming of Christ before I was almost a grown man.

So the first time I heard people talk about His coming again, I thought they were crazy. That is what the Devil wanted me to think. But the doctrine is in the Bible. It is there as clear as daylight. Jesus Christ came down from Heaven's noonday to earth's midnight. He died on the cross to save us. He was buried. The third day He rose again. Then after a while He went back up on High and is up yonder at the Father's right hand. And some day He is coming again.

One day an old preacher friend of mine was walking down a street in Philadelphia with a modernistic preacher. The modernistic preacher said, "You are looking for Jesus to come, aren't you?"

The preacher said, "Yes, I am."

"Well, do you know the difference between you and me?" said the modernistic preacher.

"What's the difference?" asked my old friend.

"Well, you are looking for Jesus and you will be disappointed. I am not looking for Him and I will not be disappointed," the modernist answered.

As quickly as a flash the old time preacher said, "There is another difference between you and me. I am doing what Jesus said to do, and you are not doing what Jesus told you to do. He told us to look for Him, and I am looking for Him." I tell you tonight, men and women, our Lord is coming back again sometime.

Christ's Second Coming Must Be a Literal Coming

The second coming of Christ is a literal coming. Let's get this clear. Some people think of the second coming of Jesus as a sort of mystical, spiritual something. It is not. His coming is to be a literal coming. Notice this; He came literally the first time. He literally went back to Heaven. He is literally coming again. I have a friend who says he can count in the Bible 152 prophecies that have been literally fulfilled. Somebody else has said there are over 300 prophecies that have been literally fulfilled. I was never very good at figures and I have never tried to count very much, but I think I personally, if I had the time, might be able to count something like 150 prophecies that have been fulfilled literally. Let's notice just a few of them.

The prophet said Jesus should be born of a virgin. That was fulfilled literally. The prophet said He would be betrayed by a friend. That was fulfilled literally. The prophet said He should be sold for thirty pieces of silver. That was fulfilled literally. The prophet said a potter's field should be bought with the price of His blood. That was literally fulfilled. If I had time I could mention many more prophecies in the Bible that have been fulfilled, not figuratively but literally.

Now if these prophecies about the first coming of our Lord and other prophecies have been fulfilled literally, why should we say that the prophecies having to do with the Second Coming are figurative? He was born into this world literally. He literally lived among men. He did not live among men figuratively. He walked around among men. He ate with men and travelled with men and talked with men. With His own blessed hands He touched human bodies. He was here literally. Then literally He went away. And literally He is coming back again.

Christ's Second Coming Is Not Death

The coming of Jesus is not death.

He is personally coming. Take this verse of Scripture: "For the Lord himself. . . ." Put the emphasis where God puts it. He does not just say, 'The Lord is coming.' "The Lord *himself* shall descend from heaven."

(And notice this is not the Holy Ghost. The Holy Ghost has already come. The power of God is here. People are preaching under the power of the Holy Ghost. Men and women are being convicted. The body of Christ is being made up. The church is being gathered in. And yet the inspired writer says, "The Lord himself shall descend from heaven.")

The second coming of Christ is not death. I used to think that when I was a boy. I somehow picked up the idea that when a man died, that was the second coming of Christ. But death is not the second coming of Christ. I want to get this idea over to you. Do you remember that when Jesus rose from the dead He said to one of His disciples, "If I will that he tarry till I come, what is that to thee? follow thou me" (John 21:22). He did not say He would tarry. He said, "If I will that he tarry . . ." They went around and said, 'John will never die. John will be alive when Jesus comes.' Now Jesus did not say he would. He said, "If I will that he tarry. . . ." He was saying, 'That is none of your business; you follow Me.'

Take this passage: "Our conversation [our citizenship] is in heaven" (Phil. 3:20). O Christian people, you do not belong in this world! You are pilgrims and strangers here. Do you ever get homesick? Do you go up the streets of Chicago and have a sort of feeling that you do not belong here? I get lonesome sometimes. I have travelled in foreign lands where I did not understand the language. The customs were not my customs. You and I are travelling in a foreign country. Our citizenship is in Heaven. We do not belong here. Just wait until someday when we get Home! Some people don't know who we are yet. They don't know how wonderful we are. They don't know how prominent we are. They don't know that we are joint heirs with Jesus Christ and that we are going to reign with Him some day. They don't realize that. "Our conversation is in heaven." Our citizenship is in Heaven. Oh, that is wonderful!

"Our conversation is in heaven; from whence also we look for the Saviour, the Lord Jesus Christ: Who shall change our vile body, that it may be fashioned like unto his glorious body." Now that word *vile* is not the best translation. This would be a better translation: 'the body of our humiliation.' The curse of sin is on your body. The curse of sin is on all creation. Paul says, 'All creation groans and travails in pain, waiting for deliverance.' The curse of sin is everywhere. The roses bloom, but they have thorns. Thorns are signs of the curse. The curse of sin is everywhere. All chords of nature are in the minor key. The wind sighs. The sea moans. There is a curse on creation, and it is on your body. Your body is under the curse. You have aches and pains. You lose your hair. Old Father Time comes up and pinches wrinkles under your eyes. You get so you have to help your legs up the steps. Your shoulders begin to stoop under the weight of the years.

I saw a man and woman going down a street not long ago. He was about sixty years of age and she was about fifty-five. The man looked as if he had given up a little. She was holding up her shoulders, looking nervously out of her eyes. She touched her husband on the shoulder and said, "Stand up straight. Everybody will think you are old!" Ah, sister, you are getting old, too. You can fight and fight but you will surrender some day. Your body is under a curse, under its humiliation. We work, but we get tired. My, my, the things we want to do! We run, but we get weary. The curse of sin is on our bodies. We are under the curse, under the humiliation; and after a while we die.

You know, I never have wanted to die. I do not like the thought of dying. I never saw a day in my life I wanted to die. I want Jesus to come. I have been active all my life. Here I am a little over six feet tall, weighing over two hundred pounds. I have been burning up my energy through the years. After a while I am helpless. I stop breathing. The doctor says, "He is gone." Then somebody comes in, opens up my veins, drains out all the blood, and pumps something artificial in there. Then they dress me. They say, "Get that tie over there, and that collar." They do not ask me anything about it. Then they comb my hair like they want it combed. Then they put a little something red on my cheeks so I will not look as if I am dead. But I am dead! After a bit they dress me as they want me dressed. Then I am picked up. One says to another, "Help me. Take hold over there." And they put me in a coffin, screw the lid down, carry me off to the graveyard and cover me up with dirt. I want to wait on myself! I do not like to be waited on! I do not want to die. I do not want to be buried. I do not want people pitching dirt in on me. (I do not want to be cremated either. When you bury a fellow, you do know where you left him.) I do not want to die! I want Jesus Christ to come. Don't tell me the second coming of Jesus Christ is death. When He comes He will break up funerals! He will take the dead out of coffins!

A Physical, Bodily Coming of Christ

The second coming of Christ is to be a bodily coming. Now let us go to that scene on the mountain. Jesus Christ was there, and He stretched His hand out to bless those there with Him. While He was blessing them—wait a minute: *while He was blessing them*, not after He was through. Oh, I am so glad He did not finish! While He was blessing them, while His hands were stretched out, He began to climb up into space. That is the most dramatic picture in all literature. There He is going up. He has been on a cross, has been buried in a tomb. Now He is standing on a mountain talking to some friends. Suddenly as He talks He stretches out His hands to bless them and as He is blessing them He goes up through space. We read those things and just pass on. Can you conceive it? Let's try to imagine we are talking to somebody who has been dead and is now alive again, and as we talk to that person he goes up through space.

As Jesus went up, the clouds parted and let Him pass. The sun, moon and stars stood to one side and saluted. He went up, and up. I suppose they who were with Him on the mountain stood on tiptoe trying to go with Him. They watched Him, and as they watched Him two men stood by in white apparel and said, "Ye men of Galilee, why stand ye gazing up into heaven? This SAME Jesus, which is taken up from you into heaven, shall so come in like manner as ye have seen him go into heaven" (Acts 1:11). Get the emphasis. Oh, the emphasis God gives to it! He did not say, 'Why are you looking up? He will come back.' He said, "*This same Jesus*, which is taken up from you into heaven, shall *so come* in *like manner* as ye have seen him go into heaven." Now, if I can find out how He went up, I will know exactly how He is coming back. Is there any way to find out how He went up? Yes, sir. I know how He went up.

You remember when He rose from the dead some disciples came to touch Him and He said, "Touch me not; for I am not yet ascended to my Father: but go to my brethren, and say unto them, I ascend [*present tense*] unto my Father, and your Father; and to my God, and your God" (John 20:17). Jesus Christ went on up to Heaven then. The Jews should have understood that. In the old dispensation when a Jewish priest started into the holy place to present the blood, if anybody touched him the blood was of no avail. Jesus Christ has shed His blood on the cross, but now He is on His way to present that blood on the altar of the sky, His blood that was shed on Calvary. He was going within the veil to present it, and He said, "Go to my brethren, and say unto them, I ascend." Later He was up in a room and said in substance, 'Thomas, you see this hand? This is the hand that wiped tears of sorrow from human faces. Thomas, this is the same hand that touched blind eyes and flooded them with light and touched deaf ears and made them to hear. This is the hand that touched the leper and chased his leprosy away. Thomas, you know this hand—this is the hand that I took to the tomb with Me when I was buried. Thomas, this is the hand that washed your feet. Thomas, touch Me. Put your hand right here. Come on. I am not a ghost. A spirit hasn't flesh and bones.'

On Calvary's cross He shed His blood. We read in Leviticus 17:11, "For the life of the flesh is in the blood." And, by the way, that is a scientific statement. You hear people talk about the Bible not being scientific! Possibly those men in those days knew nothing about the circulation of the blood. Men were studying astronomy before they understood the circulation of the blood. But back there in Leviticus we read: "For the life of the flesh is in the blood: and I have given it to you upon the altar to make an atonement for your souls: for it is the blood that maketh an atonement for the soul" (Lev. 17:11). Now on Calvary's cross when Jesus hung there and died He gave His blood. "Without shedding of blood is no remission" (Heb. 9:22). He gave His blood on the cross, His life. So do not talk about a "bloody gospel." Don't ridicule a "slaughterhouse religion."

"In the cross of Christ we glory." "There is a fountain filled with blood." So on the cross He shed His blood, He poured out His blood on the cross. When He rose from the dead He had a risen life. He had a literal body. It was a body so real He could actually sit down and eat breakfast with people. Now, Jesus Christ went to Heaven in that body. Listen to me, men and women. Let us get this fixed for all time. Oh, I shall never forget when it dawned on me as a young preacher. Jesus has never been a ghost to me from that day to this. It dawned on me one day that up in Heaven at the Father's right hand is Jesus Christ, a man who came back from the dead, a man with a body of flesh and bones. Listen, the same feet that were nailed to Calvary's cross are standing tonight on the streets of gold. Listen! The same hand that fondled the cheek of a mother is lifted up in the presence of the Father in Heaven.

He has a body of flesh and bones. He is coming back some day in that same body. You are going to see Him some day. You are going to see the same eyes and the same face that men saw when He was here. It was the same body that came out of the tomb that entered the tomb. It was a literal risen body of flesh and bones. This same Jesus who came from the dead like that and went back to the skies like that shall so come in like manner as they saw Him go.

Christ's Coming Must Be a Visible Coming

The coming of Jesus will be a visible coming. Let's notice it: "Behold, he cometh with clouds; and every eye shall see him, and they also which pierced him: and all kindreds of the earth shall wail because of him. Even so, Amen" (Rev. 1:7). I used to read that Scripture, ". . . . and all kindreds of the earth shall wail because of him. Even so, Amen." And I would say, "John, I wouldn't say 'Amen' when people are wailing." But one day I saw these words: "Beloved, now are we the sons of God, and it doth not yet appear what we shall be: but we know that, when he shall appear, we shall be like him; for we shall see him as he is" (I John 3:2). Now I say, "Even so, Amen." I am going to see Jesus some day. Every eye is going to see Him. Some are going to wail, but some of us, we who are saved, are not going to wail. We are going to be like Him when we see Him. Oh, how I would love to see Jesus! If Jesus Christ were in the heart of China I would cross the Pacific Ocean and go to the heart of China to look into His face for one second, but one day with undimmed eyes I am going to look into His holy face. I am going to see Him as He is. Say, listen; I see Him as a Saviour now with the eyes of my soul. I see Him with the eyes of my soul as my Lord and Master. But, men and women, you have never seen Jesus Christ as He really is. His glory! His glory! It is no wonder that the angels veil their faces and say, "Holy! Holy! HOLY!" It is no wonder that in Heaven clouds never gather on the sky! It is no wonder that there is no night there! He shines in that city. You will see

Him as He is—and you will be like Him if you are saved!

Years ago somebody told this story; I believe it was Dr. A. B. Simpson.

A steamboat with a pleasure party on board was going down the Mississippi River. A woman who was out on deck fell overboard. As quick as a flash a man leaped into the water and rescued her. He swam back to the boat and pulled her up with him. She stood there shivering in the wind, dripping wet. Somebody rushed up and said, "Take this wrap."

She said, "Take that wrap away. I want to look into the face of that man who saved me!"

I want to see Jesus, the One who found me when I was a little country boy at the age of eleven, the One whom I have never seen but the One I have loved all these years. I want to see Him! I wish I could have seen Him when He was a baby. He must have been beautiful. I wish I could have seen Him in the manger. I wish I could have seen a star leading the wise men to His cradle. I wish I could have seen Him when His mother and His legal father, his foster father, Joseph, took Him down to Egypt. I wish I could have seen Him at the age of twelve as He talked to the doctors of the law in the temple. I would have enjoyed watching those old wise men as they sat under the spell of His personality. I wish I could have seen Him at Jordan when He was baptized. I wish I could have seen Him on the mountaintop in the wilderness or on the pinnacle of the temple when He was tempted. I wish I could have been at the marriage supper that night and seen the look of astonishment on their faces when he changed the water to wine. I wish I could have seen Him perform some of His miracles. I should like to have been with Him at the tomb of Lazarus when He said, "Lazarus, come forth," and there walked out of that grave that dead man.

I wish I could have seen Him on the cross. I think it would have broken my heart if I had stood there that day and seen Him hanging in agony and blood. But, oh, how I would have loved Him! I wish I could have seen Him when He pulled off

His graveclothes and walked out of the tomb. I wish I could have seen Him down there that day at the shore when they saw Him this side of the grave. I wish I could have seen the astonished look on the face of Thomas when he saw the nail-prints. I wish I could have watched with that crowd when He climbed back up to His Father's house. But I would rather see Him when He comes again! The humblest Christian in this building tonight will have the glorious privilege of seeing Him come in glory some day. I shall see Him! And if He takes his nail-pierced hand and puts a crown on my head, I think I will let it stay there for just a minute because He put it there. And then I want to lift that crown from my head and put it at His feet and ask the redeemed hosts to sing

> All hail the power of Jesus'
> name!
> Let angels prostrate fall:
> Bring forth the royal diadem,
> And crown Him Lord of all.

I shall see Him! He is coming again. "This same Jesus, which is taken up from you into heaven, shall so come in like manner as ye have seen him go into heaven."

Christ's Second Coming Will Be Sudden, Unexpected

He is coming suddenly, in a moment, in the twinkling of an eye. It will not be the permeating of human society with the gospel, not the spreading of Christian influence in the world. That is not the second coming of Christ. It will be in a moment, in the twinkling of an eye. Like a flash of lightning He is coming. Oh, what a startled world there will be! What a startled Chicago, and New York, and London and Paris when He comes like that. Christians, listen! People are going to find out some of these days that we Christians were not the fools after all. Do not let them get you down. Do not let this wicked world oppress you. Keep lifting up your heads and looking up to the sky. He is coming one day, suddenly.

He is coming unexpectedly. A thing may be sudden and unexpected. I may expect a gun to shoot, and it shoots suddenly; but I expected it. The second coming of Jesus is to be both sudden and unexpected. He says, "Therefore be ye also ready: for in such an hour as ye think not the Son of man cometh" (Matt. 24:44). *"For when they shall say, Peace and safety; then sudden destruction cometh upon them, as travail upon a woman with child; and they shall not escape. But ye, brethren, are not in darkness, that that day should overtake you as a thief. Ye are all the children of light, and the children of the day: we are not of the night, nor of darkness. Therefore let us not sleep, as do others; but let us watch and be sober. For they that sleep, sleep in the night; and they that be drunken are drunken in the night. But let us, who are of the day, be sober"* (I Thess. 5:3–8). Let us be looking. Some of us are not going to be surprised. Every night for years I have gone to sleep saying, "Hasten Thy coming."

Listen, you folks who are back of this revival, every time you bring a soul to Christ you are hastening His coming. After while the last member of the bride will come in and then He will come. Our business is to work with the Holy Ghost in this dispensation to get a bride for Jesus. That is our job. That is our business. He is coming suddenly and unexpected, but not unexpected to us who know Him and love His coming.

Years ago a prominent church official in New York City said to another prominent church official in the same city, "John, let's go to this theatre tonight and see the play."

John said, "No, Bill, I do not want to see that show. I understand it is a rather dirty, vile, sensational sort of thing. I do not want to see it."

"Oh, come on; let's go," urged Bill.

"No; I do not want to go," John kept saying.

"Why don't you want to go?"

John said, "I'm looking for Jesus. He is coming some day. He might come while I was in that show, and I would not want Him to catch me there."

Listen! "Every man that hath this hope in him purifieth himself, even as he is pure" (I John 3:3). There is nothing that weans Christians from the world like the assurance of His coming. Sometime when you are inclined to love money and position and fame and worldly honors, just sit down for a few minutes and contemplate His coming.

Recently I went through a crisis in my life. We have a large enrollment in our college. We will turn away as many as two thousand students next year whom we cannot take care of. The school was already in good condition. There was no strain on us financially. We need not have taken on the burden of enlargement. There I was. What should I do: turn away two thousand people? No, put up buildings! More room for young people who desire training for Christian leadership! Oh, the blood we have sweat! The mortar in the buildings is almost made up of my blood.

Shall I take it easy? What shall I do? It is so easy to take it easy. Well, I cannot. I dare not. I would not want Jesus to catch me sitting down. I want to be working. I want to be out on the battlefield fighting for God. I do not want Him when He comes to have to say I was too lazy to work for Him.

When I was young I used to think I would take it easy some day. I have never taken it easy. All my life I have staggered under burdens that I could not have carried without God. This strain while I am here is just a little part of it. If I had nothing but this campaign—that used to be all I had—it would seem very light. This is only part of the load. But I would not want Him to come and find me sitting in an easy chair.

One day a woman in a meeting got up and testified. She said, "God saved me from a life of sin and drunkenness and debauchery. He has been better to me than anybody else." And then she sat down. A woman, prominent socially, a woman of wealth, got up and said, "Jesus has done more for me than He did for her. He saved me from the love of an easy chair." Christians, how can you take it easy? Your Lord is away. He is coming back some day. Is He going to find you busy when He comes?

Christ Is Coming for His Saints

One last point. He is coming for the saints. Let me read you these verses quickly before I close:

"*But I would not have you to be ignorant, brethren, concerning them which are asleep, that ye sorrow not, even as others which have no hope.* [He did not say for you not to sorrow. He did not say for you not to weep when loved ones die. But you do not weep as those weep who have no hope.] *For if we believe that Jesus died and rose again, even so them also which sleep in Jesus will God bring with him. For this we say unto you by the word of the Lord, that we which are alive and remain unto the coming of the Lord shall not prevent them which are asleep. For the Lord himself shall descend from heaven with a shout, with the voice of the archangel, and with the thump of God: and the dead in Christ shall rise first: Then we which are alive and remain shall be caught up together with them in the clouds, to meet the Lord in the air: and so shall we ever be with the Lord. Wherefore comfort one another with these words.*"—I Thess. 4:13–18.

He is coming back some day. He is going to raise the dead. Let me stop just a minute to say that I do not think He is going to raise all of them at the same time; but He is going to raise all the dead. Everybody who ever lived and died will sometime be raised from the dead. "Indian maidens will leap from the dust of city streets," and city skyscrapers will overturn to let Indian chiefs to judgment. Wanderers will push aside winding sheets of sand in the desert and get up. The ocean will swell and heave and out of its watery depths multiplied thousands who were buried there will come back to life. All the mummies of Egypt will come from the dead. All the dead! The battlefields of the earth will reproduce their dead. All the dead! But there will be this difference. He is going to watch over especially the tombs of His own. The dust of the saints is sacred dust. Jesus Christ died not only to redeem your soul but also to redeem your body. Somebody says, "It makes no difference to me about my body." Well, it matters to me. I have lived in this house sixty-two years. I have suffered pain. I have been restricted. I have been tied down to the earth by the law of gravitation when I wanted to be up in the stars finding out what was there. It matters to me! My body, as a Christian, is the temple of the Holy Ghost. It matters to me whether my body is raised or not.

My mother sleeps in a lonely graveyard. How many times I have felt her hand on my brow and her loving lips kissing mine. Do not tell me it does not matter whether Jesus raises the dead. It matters to me whether I ever see my mother again! I used to sit in her lap, put my arms around her and kiss her over and over. That is precious dust to me. Do not tell me it does not matter whether God raises my mother from the dead!

There is a woman here tonight whose son sleeps somewhere in the Pacific or over in Europe. She gave him to die for his country. Do not tell that mother that it makes no difference whether Jesus will raise the dead.

There is a woman here tonight—one day God reached out of Heaven and put a little baby in her arms. She held him a little while. She saw him smile one night and thought angels were making him dream. She saw tears on his cheeks, and heard him cry. A little later he died. A little coffin was brought into the home and the baby was put into it, then the little coffin was taken out yonder and put in the tomb. In the coffin was not only the baby but with the baby was buried the heart of the mother. Some nights now she wakes up and imagines she feels the little velvety chubby hand on her cheek. She wakes up startled to find it is all a dream. One day she will feel that hand. Some day that little baby's coffin will be opened in the cemetery and God will give the mother back her precious baby.

Christians, what a wonderful thing it is to be saved! We sorrow not as those who have no hope. He is coming! Some day

David will get up and ask for his harp with which to praise God. Abraham will shake the dust off his shroud and say to Sarah, "Get up, Sarah." Some day it will look like a camp meeting around some of these old country churches. But instead of the risen dead going into the churches, they will be going up into the sky. God is going to raise the dead and translate the living. All the Christians who are alive at the coming of Jesus will not die. We shall not precede those who are dead. You know, it seems to be God's way of compensating those who had to die. He says, 'Now all of you living folks wait just a minute. Hold back just a little bit. These folks had to die and I want to get them up first. Then you can join them. They had to fall at the end of the journey. They went through the valley. They struggled for breath. But you did not and I will not let you get ahead of them.' He will translate the living, translate us up into the air. Somebody says, "How is He going to do it?"

Well, He has already done it. There was a man by the name of Elijah. He and Elisha were walking along one day, talking things over. I can imagine this. Elisha said, "I do not know what we will do when you go. You've been the head of this school of prophets a long time. I don't know what we will do without you. Elijah, I would like to wear your robe."

Elijah said one of the most significant things in all the Bible: "If thou see me when I am taken from thee, it shall be so unto thee." He was saying, "I am going to be supernaturally translated. If you can apprehend the supernatural, you can wear a prophet's robe. No man is fit to wear a prophet's robe who cannot apprehend the supernatural." Suddenly there was a strange noise like chariot wheels and a strange breath like air from the wings of angels, and Elijah stepped into the chariot. Up the shining highway to Heaven he rode! He threw his mantle back and it fell on Elisha. Elijah did not die. He is up in Heaven tonight.

There was a man by the name of Enoch. A little girl said that Enoch and God had a long walk. They did. They walked and walked and walked. After a while Enoch said, 'It is getting a little late. I suppose I had better go home. Won't You go spend the night with me?'

God said, 'Enoch, we are so much nearer My home than we are yours, I believe I'll take you home with Me.' And God took Enoch by the hand and led him up to the gate.

When they got there the gates opened. There was an angelic host there, and God said to the angels, 'Show Enoch to his room. He has been my friend. He walked with Me in a wicked day when the lights were dim. Show him his room!' And God said to Enoch, 'Enoch, if you want anything, just ring for the angels. They are the bellboys up here.' Enoch did not die.

And when Jesus gets ready He is going to take us all up. I wish He would come now. I am ready. I am under the blood.

But wait a minute, just a minute, Jesus; there might be somebody else who is not. Are you saved tonight? Are you under the blood? Are you a child of God?

Chapter 5

WHAT IS A CHRISTIAN?

"And the disciples were called Christians first in Antioch."
—Acts 11:26.

*I*T IS NOT my purpose to talk to you about why they were called Christians, but I want, if I can, to try to tell you what, in the light of the New Testament, a Christian really is.

There are many strange and false ideas about what it means to be a Christian. I suppose if I should walk up and down these aisles and ask you individually, what is a Christian, I would get many different answers. Some of you would say, "People who live in a Christian country." Somebody else might say, "People who have been baptized," and someone else would probably answer, "A Christian is a man who pays his debts and does the best he can."

1. What to Be a Christian Is and Is Not

Now in the first place, a Christian is *not a person who lives in what we call a Christian country*. As a matter of fact there isn't any Christian country in the world. America is probably more nearly Christian than any other nation on the earth, but America is not a Christian country. Now don't misunderstand me. Everything we have that is really worth keeping in our country has come from the Christian religion. The Christians are the light of the world, and the salt of the earth. If all the Christians would leave America the civilization that we have would go with them; but America is not Christian, for the overwhelming majority of the people in this country are not right with God. I do not know a single city on this continent where the majority of the people are really on the side of Jesus Christ; not even a majority of the people in America belong to any church, and I tell you frankly, after having preached the gospel in most of the states of the Union, that I do not believe fifty per cent of the church members are really Christians. You can live in what you call a Christian country, and not be a Christian.

I will tell you something else. *You can join the church, be baptized, and take communion, and not be a Christian.* It is possible to stand in the pulpit and preach and not be a Christian. I think I know more preachers than any man my age in this country, as I have spent nearly my entire life in association with ministers. I believe the majority of our preachers are godly, unselfish, consecrated men of God, but nobody would tell you that every preacher in America is a saved man.

You can go to church every Sunday, and sing in the choir; and you can read your Bible every day, and say your prayers, and still not be a Christian.

You can have a Christian father and mother, and still be unsaved. I am talking to somebody now who has a mother and father who pray for you every day, and still you are living without God. There is somebody in this audience whose father and mother have gone to Heaven, and this moment they are reaching their hands through the blue sky above you and calling you to God, and still you go on in sin.

In the light of the New Testament a Christian is a person in whose life four things have taken place. If these things have not taken place in your life you are not a Christian. You may be a moral man, you may be a virtuous woman, you may have high ideals, you may have a generous heart, you may be philanthropic, you may be kind, you may be a very decent sort of a citizen, and do a great many admirable things, but unless these four things have taken place in your soul you are not a Christian.

Now what are these four things? First, conviction; second, repentance; third, conversion; and fourth, the new birth. Every man must be convicted. He must repent. He must be converted. He must be born again. I hope while I am talking you will search your heart, and ask yourself these questions solemnly, "Have I ever really been convicted for my sin, have I really and truly repented, have I been converted, have I been born again?"

I realize that it is a serious thing for me to stand here and talk to you about this subject. I am dealing with your soul. This job is more serious than the job of any surgeon in an operating room with his patient under an anesthetic. The surgeon deals with the human body. I am dealing with immortal souls. I can't afford to make a mistake. A preacher may be perfectly honest, and give the wrong directions to a lost soul.

Years ago a train with two engines attached was pulling up the mountains through the snow of the great Northwest. Aboard this train was a woman with a little baby in her arms. She had a ticket to a little town where the train never stopped except for through passengers from the East. Every time the flagman would pass through the coach this lady would say:

"Flagman, don't forget my station."

"Never mind, lady," the flagman would reply. "I'll see that you get off at the right place."

Finally a passenger, sitting across the aisle, said: "Don't worry, lady, I'll tell you when we get to the station."

At last the train stopped. The gentleman across the aisle said:

"Lady, here is your place."

She gathered up her baggage, wrapped up her baby, and got off the train hugging the baby to her bosom. A moment later the train was moving on, and in about thirty minutes it stopped again. The flagman rushed into the coach and said:

"Where is the lady who wanted to get off at this station?"

"Why she got off thirty minutes ago," said the man across the aisle.

"Did you tell her to get off?" asked the flagman.

"Yes, that was her station, wasn't it?"

"No, that wasn't any station. The engineer stopped for a

moment to repair his engine, and there isn't a house within fifteen miles of that place, and if you put that woman off there she is dead now in some bank of snow, with a frozen baby in her arms."

"My Lord," said the man, "I was honest. I thought that was her station."

"You may have been honest," responded the flagman, "but you are responsible for the death of a woman and baby."

They sent a searching party back, and sure enough they found the woman dead, hugging to her bosom the stiff, lifeless form of her little baby.

It is possible to be honest and give the wrong directions.

All I can say to you is this; I am staking my destiny for all eternity on what I am telling you.

I think I am familiar with the fundamental truths of the New Testament, and my business all my life has been to apply these fundamental truths to the human soul. You must be convicted, you must repent, you must be converted, you must be born again. You say, "Bob Jones, those are theological terms, and I don't know what they mean."

Never mind, I am going to make them simple so you can understand.

I saw it illustrated one time like this: I am walking straight down a road. I stop. I say, "I am going in the wrong direction. I ought to turn around and go the other way." The stopping is conviction. I resolve to turn around. The resolving to turn around is repentance. I turn around. The turning around is conversion. I go straight the other way and trust Jesus Christ as a personal Saviour, and then I am born again. The new birth is the divine life which is imparted to me when I, by simple faith, trust Jesus Christ as a personal Saviour. We have talked about the new birth in such strange theological terms that the rank and file of the people don't know what we mean.

I read in the first chapter of John these words:

"But as many as received Him, to them gave He power to

become the sons of God, even to them that believe on His name."

The next verse teaches explicitly that the people who thus receive Jesus are born, not of blood, nor the will of the flesh, but of God. In the First Epistle of John we read the words: "He that hath the Son hath life." If we receive Christ we have Him, and if we have Him we have life. There is just one difference between a Christian and a sinner. A Christian has Christ, and a sinner hasn't. That is a big difference. It's the difference between Heaven and Hell.

You can have religion and not be a Christian. Of course, when we speak of "getting religion" in this country, we mean becoming a Christian, but as a matter of fact everybody has some kind of religion. You can't live without religion. Man is a religious animal. That does not mean he is a Christian animal. The meanest man in this city has some sort of religion. Religion is reliance. The thing upon which you rely for salvation, that is your religion. Some men rely upon one thing, some upon another. Your religion is no stronger than your reliance. A Christian is a person who, knowing that he is insufficient in himself, that he is helpless and undone, and that he cannot save himself, relies upon Jesus Christ and His atoning blood alone for salvation. That's a Christian. He doesn't rely upon himself; he doesn't rely upon his morality; he doesn't rely upon his religion; he doesn't rely upon his church membership. He doesn't partly rely upon any of these things. He relies absolutely, unconditionally and unreservedly upon Jesus Christ.

Years ago I was standing by the deathbed of an old minister down in Alabama. The old man had been a preacher for fifty years. I saw his son, who also was a minister, kneel by his father's bed.

"Father, let your mantle fall on me," cried the son.

"Son, get the mantle of the Lord. My mantle is rags and tatters."

"But father, you have preached for fifty years, and have done more good than any man I know."

The old man, with feeble but distinct voice, said:

"Don't tell me about that, son. Tell me about the blood of Jesus. Nothing but the blood of Jesus will do for a dying man."

If a man who had preached for fifty years and who had lived a pure, straight life, in his dying hour had to rely upon the blood of Jesus Christ, don't you ever think there is any hope for you aside from this atoning blood.

> What can wash away my sin?
> Nothing but the blood of Jesus.
> What can make me whole again?
> Nothing but the blood of Jesus.

Nicodemus wasn't a drunkard or a libertine or a degenerate. If Nicodemus had lived in this city he would have been a leading figure in your moral fights and civic reforms. He would have been a member of your church and on your official board. You would have sent him as a delegate to your conventions, or your conferences, or your general assemblies. But one night Nicodemus went to see Jesus, and the holy eyes of Jesus searched the soul of Nicodemus as He said: "Except a man be born again, he cannot see the kingdom of God." Remember that Jesus was talking to the best man of his day. If you haven't been born again you may be a moral, manly man, and you may be a pure, sweet, cultured, refined, modest, virtuous woman, but you sit in that pew in darkness and in sin.

People come to me and say, "Bob Jones, do you believe in instantaneous conversion?" I tell you, there is no other kind of conversion. If you are saved there was a moment in your life when you stepped out of darkness into light, and out of death into life. You may not know when it happened. You may have gradually come up to the line, but the stepping over was instantaneous. If you have never stepped over that line, let this be the moment of your decision. Remember, you are without excuse. We are making it plain to you now. Let's review just a little. A Christian is a person who has been convicted. He has repented. He has been converted. He has been born again.

In the light of what I have said, are you a Christian? I pray God that the Holy Spirit may search your heart, and if you have not settled it, that you make your decision before you leave this building.

2. Why You Should Be a Christian

I want to give you a few simple reasons why you ought to become a Christian. These reasons are not only simple, but are very practical.

In the first place, you should become a Christian because it is right. There are two words in the English language which appeal to me tremendously. They are little words, but they are mighty big little words. These words are, DO RIGHT. I would like to write them in letters of fire, and flash them over the streets of every city, over every school door, over every office door, and over the entrance of every home.

DO RIGHT. No man ever lost in this world by doing right. He may seem to be losing. People may stand off and watch him and think he is losing, but no man ever lost in life's deal by doing right. No man ever won by doing wrong. You may watch your neighbor who is living in sin, and you may think he is winning, but just as sure as there is a just God on the throne of this universe, the man who does right is bound to win, sometime, somewhere, and the man who does wrong is bound to lose, sometime, somewhere. If you do right, you have Omnipotence back of you. If you do wrong you have Omnipotence against you.

In the first place it is right to yourself to become a Christian. I think God expects me to get the most possible out of life. I think I owe it to myself to treat myself square. I would not be square with myself if I were to turn my back on Jesus Christ and live my life in sin. What would you think of me tonight if I walked out from this service, went to my room, took a gun, and blew out my brains? You would say, "That is suicide. You are sinning against yourself." But the man who rejects Jesus Christ and lives in sin murders his immortal soul. He commits suicide for all eternity.

In the next place, you owe it to your fellow man to become a Christian. There isn't a man in this building who is so insignificant but who has some sort of influence on some other life. If you live in sin you injure the other man. It is unethical for any man to be a sinner.

Dr. George Truett, that princely pastor of the First Baptist Church of Dallas, Texas, and one of the world's greatest Christian leaders, was conducting a revival in a certain city a few years ago. Night after night two fine looking young men came into the services and took their seats near the front. They were such brilliant-looking fellows, and such attentive listeners that Dr. Truett became greatly interested in them. One day he inquired concerning them, and the pastor of the church told him that they were the two most brilliant young lawyers in the city. He learned that they were not members of any church, but that they were clean, moral, manly fellows.

One morning Dr. Truett went to the office to see these young men, and introduced himself to them.

"Gentlemen," said Dr. Truett, "I want to talk to you. I want to know why you young men are not Christians? You seem to be intelligent young men, and you have listened attentively to my sermons."

One of the young men looked into Dr. Truett's eyes and said:

"Doctor, if we were to tell you why we are not Christians you would think we are very foolish. We graduated in the same class at college, and finished our course in law together. We decided to go into partnership, and be clean, upright lawyers. We looked over this state to find us a model after whom we could pattern our lives and profession. We chose Judge Blank for our model. He is a man above reproach, and one of the cleanest lawyers in the world. We learned that he was not a member of any church and made no profession of religion. We are not unbelievers, but we are living up to our resolution to model our lives after Judge Blank."

"Young gentlemen, I am glad to have met you, and will look for you at the service tonight," said Dr. Truett as he passed out the door.

The great preacher walked over to the office of this prominent judge.

"My name is Truett, and I have come here to ask you a question in ethics. I want to know if it is right for any man to occupy a position in his community that injures his fellow man?"

"Why, certainly not," the judge replied.

Dr. Truett told him the story of his conversation with the young lawyers. The judge walked to the window and looked out at the crowd on the street for just a minute, and then, turning around he looked straight into the eyes of the preacher as he said:

"I will come out to hear you preach tonight, Doctor."

That night as Dr. Truett sat in the pulpit looking out upon the crowd he saw the prominent judge walk down the aisle and take his seat near the front. A minute later the two young lawyers came down the same aisle and found a seat just behind the judge. Dr. Truett preached on "Influence." When he was through he gave the invitation for men to come to the front and accept Christ. The influential judge came down the aisle, and just behind him followed the two young lawyers.

My friend, it is unethical for you to be a sinner. If you will come down this aisle on the invitation and take your stand for Christ somebody else will follow you. You owe it to that somebody else to take the stand.

In the third place you owe it to Jesus Christ to become a Christian. I don't understand what a man is thinking about who is willing in this day to press a crown of thorns upon the brow of Jesus. The shadow of His cross has reached down across these two thousand years. He has become the center of human history, and about His cross multiplied millions of human hearts cling. When He was dying He said, "Father, forgive them; for they know not what they do." He can't pray that prayer for you tonight because you know what you are doing. You know that you are mistreating the Son of God, and you know that you are not square with God, as long as you reject Jesus Christ.

2. *You ought to become a Christian because it is safe.* I am going to suppose that there isn't any God. I know there is a God. You ask me how I know? I will tell you. Suppose tonight when I turn off the light and get into my bed I look up through the darkness and I say, "I am thirsty; I want a drink of water," and a moment later I feel a glass of water in my hand, and I drink and quench my thirst. Tomorrow night when the darkness shuts me in I say, "I am hungry; give me something to eat." A sandwich comes to my hand, and I eat and my appetite is satisfied. Suppose that kind of thing should happen for thirty nights. If I am not a fool I would soon decide there must be an unseen personality in my room who delights to grant my request. I know there is a God. I have never seen Him, but many times He has heard my prayer. I have had a load on my shoulder pressing down upon me until I have grown so tired I could not carry it any more. I have looked up into the sky and said, "I would like to have some rest." I didn't see the hands that lifted the load, but I felt the load lifted and I found the needed rest. I have had problems to solve, and I have worked on those problems until after a while, with despair in my heart, I have looked up into the heavens and asked for help. I didn't see the God who solved them, but the problems were solved. Many times I have come to the parting of life's road, and I didn't know which way to go. I have stood still for a moment and asked for wisdom, and some unseen God gave me the wisdom.

So, I know there is a God. Remember, I am supposing, though, that there isn't any God. I am supposing this Bible is a lie, and that there isn't any Heaven, and there isn't any Hell. I am supposing that when a man dies that is the last of him. I am supposing that earth's teeming millions who have lived, and dreamed, and hoped, and died, have gone back to dust to sleep forever, and that they had no immortal souls.

When I was fourteen years old I knelt by my mother's dying bed, and promised to meet her in Heaven. A few moments later my father sobbed and said, "Son, mother is gone." The next day they took her precious body and buried it in a lonely graveyard in southeast Alabama. I have gone to that grave many times late in the afternoon, and I have sat there until the twilight shadows of the evening would fall, and the stars would come out in the sky, and I have said, "I will see my mother again." They tell me I am dreaming. If this is a dream, don't disturb me, for my religion hangs as a rainbow of hope over the dust of my dead, and kindles a smile upon the brow of my bereavement.

Let us suppose that religion is real, that there is a personal God, that the Bible is His inspired Word, that there is a literal Heaven and a literal Hell, and both are eternal. Suppose that there is a coming judgment to which every man must go, that every man who accepts Jesus will go to Heaven, and every man that rejects Him will go to Hell. If it is so I win for two worlds. If it is only a dream, I have already won. I can't lose. I have played the game safe.

3. *In the next place you should become a Christian because gratitude demands it.* Suppose I am passing through this city tonight and I see a home going up in smoke and flames. I hear a woman crying, and I notice that the staircase is burning and flames are leaping out from all the windows. I wrap something about me the best I can and rush through the stifling smoke to rescue the woman. I wrap about her some bedclothes, and come out through the smoke and flame. I put her down in a place of safety, and find that not even a hair of her head is singed. My face is scarred for life. The flesh is burned from my hands, and I rush out in the darkness without a word of

complaint. Suppose ten years from this day I am in a certain city walking down the street, and I pass a magnificent home. I walk upon the front porch and ring the bell. A lady comes to the door. I say, "Lady, I want something to eat."

"Who are you?" she asks.

"Just a plain tramp, that's all," is my reply.

"Well, where did you get those scars?" she inquires.

"Ten years ago I was in a certain town and saw a building burning. Attracted by the cry of a woman, I rushed through the stifling smoke and flames and rescued that woman and put her down in a place of safety. I noticed that not a hair of her head was singed, and there was no scar on her body, but I received that night these scars which I have carried ever since."

"Oh," she says, "stop, I am that woman. Come on in here. You can have a home as long as you live. You shall never want for food and money."

Who is that knocking outside your heart's door? It is Jesus. "Where did You get all those wounds?" I asked Him.

"On the cross," He replies.

"Your brow is pierced with many a thorn, and Your side— where did You get that scar?"

"I received all these wounds at the cross," He replies. "Two thousand years ago I laid down my life that I might save you forever." Listen to me, men and women, if there is a drop of gratitude in your blood you will accept Him. Man, if you have a heart beating under that suspender buckle you will trust Him and confess Him now. Woman, if you have a woman's soul in your body you will accept Him before you leave this building. The greatest moral monstrosity the world ever saw is a woman who can reject Jesus.

4. *One more step: You ought to become a Christian now, because of the uncertainty of human life.* You say, "Bob Jones, we have heard that many times." Yes, sir, but you ought to heed it this time. It is always today with God. It is always tomorrow with the fool.

Some months ago I was entertained for a few days in a lovely Alabama home. I liked my host as much as any man I ever saw. He was one of those bighearted, old-time, naturally lovable fellows. I just couldn't keep from loving him. He was my kind; didn't have any airs; he was just his plain, natural self. When I was ready to tell him good-by I noticed some tears in his eyes. I said, "Brother Jim, if I can ever do anything for you, I want you to let me know."

A few days later I had a letter from him. He said something like this:

"My dear friend Brother Bob: My friend, Mr. Blank, in this town, who holds a certain political position, is dying. He has sent for me and told me that he wants me to be his successor in office when he goes. Now," he said, "I don't want to be after a man's job before he dies, but I must have help if I get this position. I didn't support the present governor, and I haven't much pull with this administration. I want you to help me. Please see my friend, Mr. So-and-So, in Montgomery, and you and he go to see the governor and tell him the circumstances and try to get this position for me. I am sure my friend will be gone before this letter ever reaches you."

I answered his letter at once, telling him I would be glad to do what I could, and assuring him that I would return to Montgomery in two or three days and take up the matter with the governor. Before my letter reached my friend he fell dead! I kept up with the other man whose position he wanted, and that man was living months later.

The uncertainty of human life demands that you settle this question and settle it now. There was never a bigger lie born in Hell, or hatched in the domain of the Devil, than the statement, "You have plenty of time." "Behold, now is the accepted time: behold, now is the day of salvation."

Chapter 6

THE WOMAN IN THE CASE

"And after certain days, when Felix came with his wife Drusilla, which was a Jewess, he sent for Paul, and heard him concerning the faith in Christ. And as he reasoned of righteousness, temperance, and judgment to come, Felix trembled, and answered, Go thy way for this time; when I have a convenient season, I will call for thee. He hoped also that money should have been given him of Paul, that he might loose him: wherefore he sent for him the oftener, and communed with him."—Acts 24:24–26.

I CALL YOUR special attention to these two verses: "And after certain days, when Felix came with his wife Drusilla, which was a Jewess, he sent for Paul, and heard him concerning the faith in Christ. And as he reasoned of righteousness, temperance, and judgment to come, Felix trembled, and answered, Go thy way for this time; when I have a convenient season, I will call for thee."

Felix' First Motive—Money

Paul, the great apostle, was in jail awaiting his trial. Felix and Drusilla, a very wicked couple, sent for Paul. They had two reasons, I am sure, for sending for him. One reason is made very clear in the last verse I read. They hoped to make some money out of Paul's trouble. That is just like some people. I have known folks who would look in the bottom of the cup of human sorrow for a dollar.

I remember years ago I was out in a Missouri town in a campaign. Just across from our auditorium was a saloon, the worst saloon in town. The man who ran it, with his crowd, would be boisterous and loud and almost disturb our worship when we met for services. One night while I was preaching, the saloonkeeper was over there pointing to the auditorium and saying, "Boys, you didn't go over to the revival tonight. The preacher over there is out after money, the evangelist is preaching for money."

A fellow came in and said, "Jim, let me sweep out your saloon for a drink."

The saloonkeeper said, "All right." So he swept out the saloon. While the fellow was making fun of the meeting, he walked up to take his drink. As he picked up the glass he fell dead. Someone told me the story.

Years before, that bum was a fine businessman in the city, a princely gentleman. One day he lost his wife, a wife he loved devotedly. He had no Christian faith so he tried to drown his sorrow in the cup at the bar. He squandered everything he had for drink, lost everything he had in the world, and had come to the place where he was a miserable bum. Then he fell dead at the bar where he had taken his first drink.

I would hate to be that saloonkeeper. I would hate to be a man like that. If I were like that I would not talk about a preacher preaching for money. I thank God that I never made a dollar out of human wretchedness and human sorrow. I would hate to think that I had ever turned the widow's tears and the orphan's tears into gold. I would hate to make money by appealing to human weakness and human suffering.

Felix said, 'Let's send for Paul. He is a Jew. We can maybe get some money out of his predicament.'

The Sinner's Second Goal—A Thrill

Then I think there is another reason he sent for Paul, though it is not mentioned here in the Scripture. I think he sent for Paul because time was dragging heavily on his hands. Time always drags heavily on the hands of a sinner. I think Felix had heard of Paul, heard he was a scholar, heard he was a philosopher, heard he was a rather radical, extreme sort of man. Yet he was an interesting character. He said, 'Wouldn't you like to hear him talk? Let's send for him.' He was looking for a thrill.

I am sorry for sinners, all you men and women without God who are looking for something to delight you, something to thrill you. The trouble about it is that the thing that satisfies you today will not satisfy you tomorrow. It takes something more exciting, something more stimulating, something more exhilarating. But we who have Jesus Christ have found Him a satisfying portion.

One day a lady said to Mr. Moody, "There is a very sensational show coming to this town. People say it is a little questionable, but I would like to see it. What do you think about my going to it? What do you think about a Christian seeing that sort of thing?"

"Oh," Mr. Moody said, "I always go to a show like that when I want to."

She said, "You do!"

"Yes, Madam; but I never *want* to go. I have something much better!" Say, we Christian people have something so much better! People lose their taste for garlic and onions when they feed on heavenly manna; they do not much care for the slop that the hogs eat when they can sit down at a table and have the angels wait on them and feed on the bread of life. Oh, the poor sinners in this city, running hither and thither, looking for a thrill! I have had a real thrill, the stimulating power of God's grace, a sense of God's nearness, a consciousness of God's presence. I am sorry for you sinners. Don't you sympathize with us Christians! We are getting along fine, thank you. We are having a good time. You are tossed about upon a restless, disturbed sea; we have calm that you know nothing about.

Paul Had Seen a Vision, and Nothing Could Stop Him

Felix said, 'Let's send for Paul,' and Paul comes into the presence of that wicked couple. Let's you and me coach him a little; let's tell him how to preach. "Now, Paul, you have a very prominent man in the audience, and a prominent woman. You are in jail. You are going to have a trial before long. Now, listen, Paul, you can make up to that couple. Here is your chance! Sell yourself to them. Try to sell yourself. Flatter them a little. Say some nice things to them. You can win them, and they will be eating out of your hand. When your trial comes up they will get you out. This is the opportunity you have been looking for."

But Paul was not like that. Paul forgot himself. He stood in the presence of this wicked couple and preached the truth to them. He dared to preach the truth. Say, all Hell could not stop Paul! It did not matter what people did to him; they could not stop him. He did not mind a jail. I said the other day that if you built a prison across Paul's path, he would walk through the prison and come out on the other side with a convert under one arm and a prison gate under the other. Nobody could stop him. When Paul was preaching in a town he never did say, "I wonder what kind of hotel is in that town?" He said, "I wonder what kind of jail they have in that town. Say, Silas, were you ever in that place? What kind of dungeon was there?" Nobody could stop Paul. One day he was going down the road to Damascus and he saw a light flash from Heaven. He heard a voice out of eternity, and he never forgot it. When the sun comes up, the stars always hide. I met a man not long ago who told about his scholarship and his degrees—all about his experiences and how much he knew. How he did strut his stuff! He was a preacher, too. I thought to myself, "Brother, how many people did you ever win to Jesus Christ?" What good does a D.D. and an LL.D. and a Ph.D. do; what good does a university diploma and a seminary diploma do if you have never won anybody to Jesus Christ? What good is all the knowledge that men can give you unless you use it for God? A Christian has no right to anything he does not use for God. You have no right to scholarship unless you use it for God. You have no right to money unless you use for God. You have no right to health unless you use it for God. A Christian has no right to *anything* he does not use for God! The only business a Christian has of getting is to get so he can serve. The more you know, the more responsibility you have.

People could not stop Paul. He had a vision. That day he met Jesus he forgot about his diploma. He forgot he was a D.D. He forgot that he was a blue-blooded aristocrat. He forgot about his ancestors. He said, 'Since I met Jesus Christ all these things amount to nothing to me. They sink into absolute insignificance.' I find that the more men know about God, the less they magnify some things that some folks magnify.

Let's suppose that you and I were living back in Paul's day. One day you are going down the road to Damascus and you see a little man running down the road. You say, "Hello, Mister. What are you running for?"

"Oh," he says, "they are about to kill me!"

"About to kill you? What have you done?"

"I was up there and some friends put me in a basket, took a rope, and let me down over the wall. If they had not done it, I suppose I would have been killed. But I am about to get away."

"Well, what did you do? Were you in jail?"

"Oh, no, no!"

"You didn't kill anybody?"

"Oh, no, no!"

"Well, what are you running for?"

"Well, I will tell you how it was. I was up there preaching. I was telling the people that God loved them and Jesus died for them, and they did not like it. They said, 'Let's kill him! Let's kill him!' And they would have gotten me if somebody had not put me in a basket, taken a rope and let me down."

"Now, wait a minute, Mister. You talk like you've been to school. I believe you are a university graduate. You talk like a scholar. Don't tell me you've gone off with those fanatics.

Say, you have a background; you have scholarship; you have standing!"

But Paul says, "Gentlemen, you don't understand. One time I was going down to Damascus, and I saw a light flash from Heaven. I heard a voice out of eternity, and I have been in debt ever since that time. I must pay the debt."

You say, "Poor fellow, isn't it strange that a man with his intelligence and sense and background would go off on a tangent like that, act the fool and be a warped man, a fanatic —isn't it a pity?"

Somebody answers you, "Well, you can't ever tell how a fellow is going to turn out, you know. Things like that happen. Here we are going along in the middle of the road, sane, and making some money."

Time passes and one day on the outskirts of the city you see some dogs and boys. You say, "What's the matter, boys?"

One of the boys says, "Well, Mister, I don't know; but it looks to me like this fellow is dead. I believe he's dead as sure as the world!"

You get off your horse, go over there and lay your head down on his chest. You say, "No, no; he's not dead. His heart is beating. Son, run get me some water. Hurry! I believe the fellow is alive, and we may be able to save him."

The little boy runs and brings some water. You wash the dirt off of his face. He opens his eyes and says, "Glory to God! Hallelujah! Praise the Lord!"

You say, "He's out of his head. He has a high fever and is raving."

He says, "No, I'm not out of my head. Hallelujah!"

"What's the matter?"

"They left me for dead. I thought I was about gone, too. Listen, I've been so close to Heaven that I was kissed by spirits from a world celestial, and was fanned by zephyrs from the wings of angels, and read my titles clear to mansions in the sky!"

"What is your name? What are you talking about? What are you raving about?"

Paul says, "I beg your pardon. My name is Paul."

"Paul? Why hello, Paul! We met you one time coming down the Damascus road. We knew something was going to happen to you. Why do you want to be crazy like that, go off on a tangent and take up with that crowd of fanatics?"

Paul says, "By the way, did I tell you gentlemen about that day I was going down the Damascus road and saw a light flash from Heaven and heard a voice out of eternity? I just want to tell you that I am in debt. I have a debt to pay, and I am going to try to pay it. Will you help me to my feet? I believe I can stand alone if you will help me up. I am going to get to preach some more—hallelujah! I'm going to get to tell somebody else that God loves them and Jesus died for them."

You say, "Good-by, old fellow; it is too bad."

We go on off and talk it over. We talk about how wise we are and about how little sense he has.

One day we get aboard a vessel to go over to Macedonia. We are about to sit down when we see a fellow come aboard. I say, "By the way, that guy looks like . . . Say, Mister, wait a minute! Isn't your name Paul?"

"Yes, gentlemen. How are you? I am glad to see you."

"Where are you going?"

"I am going over to Macedonia to preach. I got a call from over there last night."

"Didn't anybody speak to the committee . . . "

"No, while I was sleeping the angel of the Lord stood by me and said, 'I want you to go to Macedonia.' And I'm on the way over there to preach the gospel and tell the glorious story of God's love and God's redeeming grace."

"Now listen, Paul, I want to talk to you. You are just crazy, that's all. A man of your intelligence wasting your time like that! We have a bank over in Macedonia, and we need a good, honest, upright man—a man of culture, a man who can speak several languages. We will pay you a big salary."

Paul says, "That is very kind of you, gentlemen—say, by the way, I believe I told you fellows about that day I was going down to Damascus and the light I saw flash from out of eternity. I am going over to Macedonia to help pay the debt."

We say, "Oh, you can't do anything with him; he's crazy!"

Time passes, and one day we are going down a road. As we draw near to a city we see people leading some prisoners off down a road for execution. In the front ranks is a little Jew with steady step. I say, "You know, that little fellow looks like that Jew, Paul. Say, Mister, what is your name?"

"My name is Paul."

"Why, hello, Paul!"

"Hello, gentlemen."

"Where are you going, Paul?"

"I'm going to Heaven in a few minutes."

"What's the matter?"

"They're cutting my head off."

"Why, Paul—what's the matter! Is there anything we can do for you?"

"No, no! Thank you very much, gentlemen. You've been very kind, but there is nothing you can do."

"Well, we're awfully sorry, Paul. We really have an affection for you. We thought you were crazy but there is something about you that commanded our respect and stirred our affections. We wish we could do something for you, Paul."

"By the way, did I tell you gentlemen about the day I was going down the road to Damascus and the light I saw flash from Heaven and that voice out of eternity? I want to tell you I have the debt paid. I have written Timothy a letter and told him I fought a good fight, I finished the course, I kept the faith. The debt is now all paid. I am ready to be offered."

You know, all Hell cannot stop a man like that! Guns cannot stop him. Jails cannot stop him. Kings on their thrones cannot stop him. Nothing can stop him!

Paul Dared to Preach the Truth

That was the man who stood in the presence of this wicked couple and preached the truth to them. He dared to preach the truth to them. He did not preach love to them. I believe it was Gipsy Smith who said, "We have preached love in this country until some people are lovesick." Do you know what this country needs? This country needs six months of Hell-fire and damnation preaching. This country needs the righteousness of God and the justice of God preached. We have turned God Almighty and Jesus Christ into sickly senti-mentalists. We need some old-time Jonathan Edwardses turned loose in this country. We are a bunch of egomaniacs strutting our way to Hell, thinking we are too respectable to be damned! Of course, we ought to preach love to the right crowd. It is all right to tell a sinner that God loves him if you put the rest of it in there, too; but this thing of standing up and just telling sinners God loves them, and never telling them that sin damns them and that God is a just God, is not enough and you had better watch out if you are doing it.

I have always preached love to some people. I never preach Hell to a drunkard. You do not have to preach Hell to a drunkard. There is not a drunken bum in Chicago who wants to be a drunkard. There never was a drunken bum who ever staggered down the street who wanted to be that. He is a poor, helpless slave. Tell him that God loves him. Tell him that Jesus Christ died for him. But do you know who needs Hell preached to them? These frizzly-headed, cigarette-smoking, cocktail-drinking society women! These respectable folks who have their cocktail parties and think they are too decent to go to Hell—that is the gang that needs it! I never preached Hell to a harlot in my life. I have been in those homes of shame with the gospel, those places where the soiled doves of the underworld live in their infamy. You do not have to preach Hell to a harlot. She knows more about Hell than any preacher can tell her. No woman at heart wants to be that. I talked to one in a West Virginia city whose own dear uncle was president of one of the greatest universities in America. She told me the story of how she made her first wayward step. As I stood there with those prominent Christian women (she had requested to see a preacher) and told her God loved her, she said, "Not me. Not me!"

I said, "God loves you."

But do you know who needs Hell preached to them? These women who are running to the divorce courts every week, getting a divorce on every little excuse, breaking marriage vows—this high-society, godless, worldly, sensual gang! The high-brows are the ones who need it! Jesus Christ never preached Hell to the sin-sick and world-weary. He told them about a prodigal son, a lost sheep and a lost coin. But those godless Pharisees he called a generation of vipers and said, 'How can you escape the damnation?'

Paul talked straight. He did not review the latest book. Nothing makes me so sick as to find some preacher on a Sunday night looking at empty pews and reviewing the latest book when he has the Word of God to preach—THE WORD OF GOD, the power of God!

Paul did not try to match wits with people. I have no patience with that either. A man said the other day, "When you get to talking to these university people, match wits with them. Do not use the term *new birth* because they will not know what you are talking about."

I said, "Jesus Christ used the term *new birth* to a man and told him he could not understand it."

Paul matched the Word of God against them. He reasoned of righteousness, temperance and judgment. He preached straight to them. He did not flinch. He did not dodge. He did not trim. He did not cut the message. And he preached to prominent people. Anybody can preach to the common folks, ordinary everyday people.

Years ago Peter Cartright, that pioneer circuit rider who rode his one-eyed horse across this country, that preacher who wore out his Bible and his saddle going from place to place preaching the gospel, came to Nashville, Tennessee, to a great Methodist conference. The Methodist conference would not preach him because he was a sort of a woodsman and countryman and Nashville was quite a high-brow city. It was called "The Athens of the South." They had some aristocratic people there and an aristocratic pastor, and they would not use him. People tried to get them to preach him. At last the Presbyterian pastor said, "If you will not preach Peter in the Methodist church, I will preach him in the Presbyterian church." The Baptist pastor said, "If you will not have him, we will have him in the Baptist church." At last the aristocratic Methodist preacher had to take him. Peter Cartright got up in the pulpit. He opened his Bible and started to read. As he started to read, the Methodist preacher behind him pulled his coat tail and whispered, "Peter, Peter."

Peter said, "WHAT? What do you say? You say General Jackson has just come in? Well, what do we care about General Jackson. Let me alone! If he does not repent he will go to Hell just like everybody else. Don't bother me!"

The next day General Jackson said, "Peter, come over and have dinner with me."

The next day they sat down together and General Jackson said, "Peter, if I could man my army with men like you, I could go across the Atlantic Ocean and take over the British Empire." The mightiest things on earth are preachers who will not flinch! There is no place on earth where a man is more tempted to compromise manhood than in the pulpit, and there is no place on earth where there is a greater opportunity to be a man than in the pulpit.

Paul Was Not Influenced by the Power and Position of His Audience

Paul preached to prominent people.

Years ago down on the seashore at Biloxi, Mississippi, one of those old-time camp meetings was in progress. The preacher was calling mourners up for prayer. Down the aisle came an influential Louisiana colonel. He got down on his knees but did not even bow his head. He looked at the common people around him crying. He looked around as if to say, "Now, God, if you want to save me, I'll let You do it. It will be quite a compliment to You—I'm Colonel So-and-So from New Orleans. If You save me it will be quite an honor to You. It will attract a lot of attention. If it is any favor, it is all right—I will let You do it."

The preachers would speak in an easy, at-home way to the plain people, but to the colonel they would say, "Now, Colonel, trust the Lord."

Somebody else would come by timidly and say, "God bless you, Colonel."

Another person would come by and say, "Turn loose, Colonel."

Another one would come by and say, "Hold on, Colonel."

There was a little preacher on the platform twisting around and looking at the sight. After a while he ran down there, stuck his face right under the nose of the old fellow and said, "Say! You know Bill Smith in New Orleans who has been in jail a hundred times?"

"Y—e-s. Yes, I know him."

"You are a lot meaner than he is and your Hell will be hotter than his."

"W—h-a-t do you mean?"

"I mean what I say, Sir. You impudent, God-defying rebel! Here you are—you were brought up in a good home. You had a Christian mother and every other advantage in the world. And here you are not even humble enough to bow your guilty head and say, 'God, be merciful to me a sinner.' "

The old colonel began to tremble like a leaf in the wind. He said, "God, be merciful to me a sinner!"

Let me tell you something: when some people stand at the judgment bar of God, they will have better excuses than you have. Some of you in this house tonight have had every chance to be right with God. Listen! The hottest places in Hell are going to be saved for high-brows.

I have a lot of faults. I am just as human as anybody. I am too human. If God Almighty had not saved me I do not know where I would have been. But I am going to boast a little. I know I am boasting. I am in the pulpit, but I am going to boast. I have done a lot of things I should not have done; I have made a lot of mistakes. I have blundered many a time. But I have been preaching the gospel for forty-seven years— ever since I was fifteen I have been on this job. If I had to die tonight I could stretch my hands across my breast and turn my dying, staring eyes in the face of God Almighty and tell Him that I never trimmed my message. I am not afraid to meet God on that. I have not always known what to say. I have not always known as much as I should have known. I have not prayed as much as I should have prayed. I have come short in a thousand ways. But, God Almighty, You know that when I have stood up to preach everybody has looked alike to me. The rich and the poor, the high and the low—all have looked just alike.

Listen! I want to tell you tonight—I do not care who you are—if you are not right with God Almighty you will die some day and go to Hell. I do not care how respectable you think you are! You have to repent or be damned. You have to repent or perish! You have to trust Jesus Christ or go to Hell! And you had better face it!

Paul stood in the presence of this wicked couple and preached straight to them. He did not preach love to them; he reasoned of temperance, righteousness and judgment to come. They had a chance to hear. Felix had a chance, and

Drusilla had a chance. And Paul had a chance to preach. He had to go to jail to get that chance, but it was worth going to jail to preach a fellow like Felix under conviction. You know when you preach a man under conviction—if you do not do any more than that you have done your duty. Some people say, "Preach them into the kingdom." You should preach them into a state where they will never be happy outside the kingdom!

Felix and Drusilla Had a Chance to Be Saved

Paul had a chance to preach and Felix and Drusilla had a chance to be saved. How good God is to give a man a chance. Suppose you had been born on some island where you could never have seen a Bible. You ought to be on your face, saying, "Thank You, O God, for ever giving me a chance. Thank You that I ever saw a Bible. Thank You that I ever heard anybody preach. Thank You I ever heard a church bell ring. Thank You I ever saw a gospel tract." The gospel is going out over the air today to more people than have ever heard it before. There are more people hearing the gospel in this country than ever heard it before. Listen! Millions and millions of people today are hearing the Bible preached. They are having a chance. They are hearing the gospel. The gospel is the power of God unto salvation to every one that believeth—it does not matter whether you preach it in church on Sunday morning, whether you preach it over the radio, whether you put it out by tract, or word of mouth. It is the power of God, the dynamite of God, the nitroglycerin, the high explosive of God. It is the power of God! And you have heard it.

But After a Chance, After Conviction, Judgment Must Finally Come

Felix sat there that day in the presence of Paul, the great preacher, and listened to the gospel. He was convicted. He knew that he was a sinner.

In the old days when I began my evangelistic career, people would stay awake all night. They could not sleep. I have had them call me at all hours of the night. I have known them to wake up people all over the town and say, "Pray for me." May God Almighty bring back old-time conviction in this country! In those old days we said, "This is right and that is wrong." We had definite convictions about right and wrong. And we believed there was a Heaven and a Hell. Listen! All this modern talk about not believing there is a Hell is because people have quit believing in sin. A man who believes in sin knows there is a Hell. You do not have to tell me there is a Hell. I have seen ten thousand hells on earth that were produced by sin. When I was a little boy at the age of eleven, I knew there was a Hell. I knew that was where I deserved to be. I used to slip out into the woods, get on my knees, and say, "O God, if I am not too big a sinner, please save me." I was a little country boy. I had never seen an automobile, but I had heard the music of the birds in the treetops and the songs of the wind in the forest. Everybody was decent. There was not a bad woman in that country. People were moral and clean and respectable. I saw myself a sinner. I would stay awake at night and say, "O God, maybe I am too wicked a sinner, but if I'm not, be merciful to me." Yet we have middle-aged people in this house tonight who think they are too respectable to be damned. We have to plead with you and beg you to get you to see that you are really lost. Listen, you just do not know what a sinner you are. O God, hold back Thy wrath. Hold back Thy wrath!

Let me tell you something! God Almighty will not put up with everything. You get this straight! "He, that being often reproved hardeneth his neck, shall suddenly be destroyed, and that without remedy." Do not get the idea that God Almighty will stand just anything. He will not do it!

Years ago there lived down South an old-time aristocratic southern gentleman. He had a cultured, refined wife and one boy. He put all the love of a father's heart back of that boy.

He put him through high school, and then sent him to university. The boy got drunk and was expelled. The father got him in another institution. Again he got drunk and was expelled. He got him in a third one. Again the boy got drunk and was expelled. People in the neighborhood said, "If he were my boy I would kick him out of the house." The old man went ahead. He had enough influence to get him in a fourth institution. But again he got drunk and was expelled. Then no other institution would have him. The boy came home. He would go downtown and get drunk and they would lock him up. The old man would go pay his fine, get him out, bring him home, put him to bed, and the mother would bathe him with her tears and nurse him sober. They would get him on his feet and then he would go back to town and get drunk.

One day somebody said to the father, "If that were my boy . . ."

The father said, "Don't say that! Don't say that! He is our only boy. My wife and I have talked it over. We are going to stick to him to the end, and we are not going to tolerate anybody's saying anything. You are our neighbor and our friend, but don't say anything."

One time the boy went downtown and stayed a day or two. The wife said, "Dear, you had better go get our son." The old man got a colored boy, hitched his horse to the buggy, drove downtown, hitched his horse in the wagon yard and started around to the calaboose where he expected to find the boy. He met the boy staggering along the sidewalk cursing. He came up and looked at his father and said, "What are you doing here? Go on back home and let me alone." And he spat in the old man's face. The father wiped the spittle off. Tears came in his eyes and rolled down his cheeks. The boy walked up and spat in his face again. The man wiped it off again. Then the boy hit his father and knocked out some of his teeth. The old man, with drooping shoulders, turned back and with trembling hands untied his horse. He drove back home, gave the horse to the colored boy who was there working around the

house. The man did not say a word. He went up in front of
the house into a grove and propped his feeble old form, in
which there was a broken heart, against a tree. He stood there
and cried like a baby. Then he stood back and gave an unearthly scream. He went back and stood by the tree thirty
minutes longer, trembling and sobbing and crying. Then he
threw himself back and gave the most unearthly scream ever
heard fall from human lips. He turned and went back home.
He went up on the front porch and walked up and down. He
turned his eagle eye up the road—didn't say a word to anybody.

After a while he saw the son stagger up to the gate, saw
him thumb with the latch until he got it open, and then saw
him stagger down the walk and up to the front steps. The
father waited until he reached the top step. Then he caught
him by the collar and shook him and kicked him off the porch.
He said, "Get off these premises, and don't you dare to come
back!"

In forty-eight hours that boy died with delirium tremens
and the old man would not attend his funeral.

Let me tell you something: God is sensitive. God loves!
Oh, how much He loves! He loved you so much He sent His
Son to come down to earth to die, and you spit in His face.
You strike back at His love and tenderness, and then expect
God to let you live. Listen! You had better quit playing with
God Almighty like that. You had better quit it! You had
better listen to me—you men and women who are not right
with God!

"When It Is Convenient . . ." —The Delay of Sin

Felix—that poor, wicked, depraved degenerate—was decent enough to tremble. He said, 'It isn't convenient, Paul.'

It isn't convenient? What is the matter with you, Felix?
What is the matter with you?

"I do not like the way Paul preaches."

Shut up! Shut up!

You say, "I don't want to come to God in a revival." Well, why didn't you come when you weren't in a revival?

You say, "That is not my way." No, your way is a Hell-bound way. Don't strut your stuff around some of us who have enough sense to know what is the matter with you!

"What is the matter, Felix?"

"I can't believe." Shut up! You old liar—shut up! Listen! a preacher said to me, "The Lord has called me to preach to honest doubters." There are no honest doubters. Jesus settled that. He said, "If any man will do his will, he shall know of the doctrine, whether it be of God, or whether I speak of myself." God Almighty did not ask you for your head. What does He want with it! He said, "Give Me your heart." If you will give Him your heart He will comb all the kinks out of your head. Your trouble is not in your head; it is in your heart.

The Woman in the Case

It is not convenient. What is the matter, Felix? Let me tell you what is the matter with him. He has a sin in his life. Drusilla was not his wife by rights. She really belonged to another man. She was the woman in the case. He was living in adultery. He came where the road parted and there was his woman and here was Jesus. He knew he ought to go with Jesus, but he was in the clutches of a woman. He stood there between the two trembling.

It was a woman who robbed Samson of his strength. That mighty man—with his head in the lap of Delilah! It was a woman whose voluptuous dance sent Herod to Hell, and Herod is not the only man who was ever sent to Hell by the voluptuous dance of a woman. It was a woman who stood in the gate of Heaven and shoved Felix down to Hell. Listen! There are millions of men being damned by women! The best thing outside of Heaven is a good woman, and the meanest thing outside of Hell is a mean woman! We talk about men and women living on the same plane. They do not. Women have more soul than men. They are always a little above or a little beneath men. There are more girls seducing boys in America than there are boys seducing girls. There was a time in this country when thinking mothers said, "How can I protect my good girls from bad boys?" Now in America intelligent mothers are saying, "O God, help me to protect my boys from bad girls." In Bob Jones College in normal times we have about as many girls as we do boys, about fifty-fifty. I will match the purity of my boys against the purity of my girls in Bob Jones College. Men in this country, as a whole, are just as good as women. That was not so twenty-five years ago. The percentage of good men, I think, has been slightly on the increase. But the percentage of good women year by year has been on the decrease. No nation ever went to Hell until its women went to Hell. There might be some hope for America if all men were bad and the women good. But there would be no hope for this nation if all men were good and all women were bad. Listen! Don't you mothers blame the world—you had the babies first. You put your stamp on them before the world ever got them. You taught them to lisp their first baby words. You saw them make their first little steps. A man can go to Hell with a good mother, but it is not easy to do so. Oh, the grip of a woman's power over a man! I saw a man in this meeting three nights ago under conviction. He sat beside a woman. If she had come, he would have come with her. There are women in this house whose menfolks would come to God if they would come to God. Your sweetheart would come to God if you would come to God.

Felix trembled. The Bible does not say that Drusilla trembled. You would have thought it would have been Drusilla, but it was not.

There they sat. I can see her. She is not moved. But Felix is trembling as he says, 'It isn't convenient, Paul. It isn't convenient. I'll send for you later. If it ever gets convenient, I'll send for you. Go on back to jail, Paul.'

I can hear Paul's footfalls and the rattle of his chains as he goes on back to jail. Back to jail, thou man of God! Back to jail, thou hero of the cross! Back to jail! I would rather wear your prison chains than the chains of passion and the slavery that bind Felix. Go on back to jail. Go on back, Paul; we will never forget you. Two thousand years hence a preacher in the Arena in Chicago will be telling people how you preached. You have given all the preachers of all generations an example of heroism. Go on back, Paul—back down the corridor, back to jail, thou wonderful man of God! (Footfalls heard as Paul goes back to jail.) You chose to suffer rather than to compromise. Go on back, Paul! Go on back! He went on back down the corridor, inside the cell, and the door was closed. And the door that shut him in, shut Felix out.

You Must Decide Now—Choose Jesus or Your Sin

I believe that was the day of destiny for Felix. I believe that across every sinner's path God Almighty draws a deadline. On one side there is hope; on the other side there is death. That deadline is possibly at the door of this building for somebody tonight. If you go out without God after facing this hour, it may fix your destiny for eternity.

I have learned that a sinner may have many sins, but every sinner has one sin that dominates him, one king sin, one sin on the throne, one big sin. There is always, in every case I have ever found, some one sin in the sinner's way; and when that one goes, the others go. You may have a thousand sins, but if you are not a Christian there is some one thing tonight in your way. It may not be a woman or a man. It may be intellectual pride. It may be selfish ambition. It may be a strange love of pleasure. It may be something that I do not even think to mention; but if you are a sinner, tonight you are where the road parts. Here is Jesus on one side and here is sin on the other side. And you are going to make a choice tonight. Everybody in this house is going to make a choice. Jesus is here. You are going to make a choice.

Wait a minute! The recording angel has his pen in his hand. He is going to write the choice of every one of us down.

"Recording angel, put mine down, will you? Yes, I am willing for you to write it. Put it down, 'Bob Jones.' Yes, that is the name. Write it down—poor, weak man—yes; ten thousand faults—yes; blundered thousands of times—I know it. Yes, I know it all. Blundering, miserable, helpless, human—yes, I know; but write it down: 'I choose Jesus. Jesus first'—put it down."

O Jesus, hold back the hand of the recording angel tonight and give somebody here a chance. Somebody in this house tonight has come to where the road parts. Help them to choose, Jesus.

Now every head bowed; every eye closed. I want to ask you something. There is not going to be any dodging tonight. My business as a preacher is to take every sinner's blood off my hands and throw it back on his own soul. I have not done my duty as a preacher until I leave everybody in my audience without excuse.

Prayer: Blessed Jesus, I have done the best I could. You have helped me tonight. I have felt Thy presence. The people have listened. Thou art here. O Lord God, save us from being shams and humbugs and hypocrites and liars and fourflushers. Help us to be true, God.

Men and women, let's play this game square with God tonight. I want to know how many people in this house tonight can say—think it over before you say it—"If I know my heart, I am right with God tonight."

Chapter 7

THE FAMILY RECORD

"There was a certain rich man, which was clothed in purple and fine linen, and fared sumptuously every day: And there was a certain beggar named Lazarus, which was laid at his gate, full of sores, And desiring to be fed with the crumbs which fell from the rich man's table: moreover the dogs came and licked his sores. And it came to pass, that the beggar died, and was carried by the angels into Abraham's bosom: the rich man also died, and was buried; [*It does not say anything about the beggar's being buried. The rich man was buried. There are a great many things more important than a big funeral.*] *And in hell he lift up his eyes, being in torments,* [*I want you to notice that* s *on that word. It is not just torment, but torments.*] *and seeth Abraham afar off, and Lazarus in his bosom. And he cried and said, Father Abraham, have mercy on me, and send Lazarus, that he may dip the tip of his finger in water, and cool my tongue; for I am tormented in this flame. But Abraham said, Son, remember that thou in thy lifetime receivedst thy good things, and likewise Lazarus evil things: but now he is comforted, and thou art tormented. And beside all this, between us and you there is a great gulf fixed: so that they which would pass from hence to you cannot; neither can they pass to us, that would come from thence. Then he said, I pray thee therefore, father, that thou wouldest send him to my father's house: For I have five brethren; that he may testify unto them, lest they also come into this place of torment. Abraham saith unto him, They have Moses and the prophets; let them hear them. And he said, Nay, father Abraham: but if one went unto them from the dead, they will repent. And he said unto him, If they hear not Moses and the prophets, neither will they be persuaded, though one rose from the dead."*—Luke 16:19–31.

$\mathcal{M}$Y FRIENDS, I am not going to talk to you tonight about the future life. I plan to speak Friday night on Heaven. I believe in Heaven. I believe Heaven is a literal city foursquare. I like to talk about Heaven because that is my home. I do not belong down here. I am just passing through this country on my way to my heavenly city, and I want to talk to you Friday night about my Home. Some people say we do not know much about Heaven. But if you listen to God's Word you know a great deal about it. The trouble with most of us is that we just do not take God's Word for what it says.

There Is a Hell!

I am not going to talk much about Hell tonight. I want to apologize to you for going through this series of two weeks' meetings without preaching about Hell. I do not think any evangelist does his duty until he preaches on Hell at least one time in a campaign. I believe in Hell. I speak reverently: If there is not a Hell, there ought to be one. I cannot conceive of a just God's not having a Hell for bad people. If there is a place for good people, there must be a place for bad people. If my mother is in Heaven, there must be a Hell, because my mother would not be happy with the company she would have to have if all the harlots and the degenerates and the thugs and the murderers and the blasphemers and all the Christ-rejecting sinners were around her. Nobody who is right with God could be happy in Heaven if all around him were all the wicked people in the world. If there is a Heaven for saints, I am sure there must be a Hell for sinners.

I am talking to a man tonight who years ago wormed your way into the confidence of a woman and little by little broke down her resistance. After a while you lifted from her brow the diadem of her purity and then sacrificed her on the altar of your lust. After you did that she turned her tear-stained face into yours and asked for your protection. But you went away and left her in her shame. She has been an outcast from that day to this. She is a soiled dove of the underworld if she is still alive, and you are a respectable man. Do you mean to tell me there is no Hell? Listen! If God Almighty is a just God—and I am speaking reverently—if God Almighty is a just God He will take a pen of fire some day and paint a picture of that tear-stained face on every wall in Hell. And you will see that face forever. Things must be made even. They are not even now. They are uneven in this world. A just God must fix it up some day. I believe in Hell. I hate to think about Hell, but there is bound to be a Hell. I do not see how anybody could even think and not believe in Hell.

I will tell you something else: I do not see how anybody could believe the Bible and not believe in Hell. If there is not a Hell—I am speaking reverently—this Bible is a "flaunting lie." If I did not believe in Hell I would be in favor of erecting a monument to the memory of Voltaire and Tom Paine and Bob Ingersoll and the rest of the infidels who have cursed this world.

I will tell you something else: I do not see how anybody can believe in atonement without believing in Hell. If your sins, when they were laid upon the Son of God, caused Him to bow His head and die, if your sins broke the heart of Jesus Christ on Calvary, your sins, unpardoned, will damn your soul in Hell.

I will tell you something else: I believe in a literal Hell. "Oh," you say, "Bob Jones, you don't think Hell is literal, do you? You don't think there is such a thing as literal fire in Hell?" Why not? What do you know about fire? We talk so wise but know so little! I read in the Bible about a bush that was burning but was not consumed. How do you know what kind of fires God may kindle? Yes, I believe in a literal Hell of fire.

We used to have down South a famous old preacher. He died before I was born, but I have a volume of his sermons. The old preachers down South talk about him, and I read some of his sermons. Four sermons he preached on Hell. And I remember one or two things he said about Hell. In one of his sermons, after laying his predicate and building upon it, he said, 'Hell may be a lonely, barren, desolate world, rolling beyond the confines of creation; with no sun or star to light up its darkness and chase away its infernal vapors; with oceans and rivers of liquid fire and continents of incinerated rocks, rent with awful caverns. Over it the damned may walk and climb and stumble and fall forever. There may be a law of gravity which binds the lost to its surface and holds them there forever and ever.'

But that may not be Hell. Hell may be a blasted and God-cursed planet. Rocks and mountains are tumbled into anarchy. There are no blushing flowers and laughing streams, no gospel preaching, no friendships, no morality and no God. All clans and sexes are herded with foulest demons in one promiscuous mob. Every stinking cave is inhabited with gnashing ghost and howling fiend.

But that may not be Hell. Hell may be a cavern in the heart of some God-cursed planet. In this awful cavern of woe ravens of despair may sit upon the crags and wail while God's awful justice pours His whip upon the backs of the damned forever and ever. The door to this cavern may be closed and the key tied to the girdle of God and divine Omnipotence installed to guard the way forever.

But that may not be Hell. Hell may be just a lake of fire. Did you ever stop to think about the awful horrors of a lake of fire? Think of an ocean of fire, with waves of liquid fire beating on the eternal shores and with bubbles on these waves bursting and emitting fumes in whose ascending volumes there are serpent flames.

But, sinner, you do not have to go to Hell. Please don't go. God does not want you to go. Remember He "so loved the world, that he gave his only begotten Son, that whosoever believeth in him should not perish, but have everlasting life."

God Keeps the Records of the Family

But my subject tonight is not Hell. Jesus in this story I read to you from the sixteenth chapter of Luke gives a family record. He tells some very interesting things about an interesting family.

When I was a boy in the country we had an old family Bible. Between the Old and the New Testament we kept the family record. We kept the dates of births and marriages and deaths. I used to get the record down sometimes and look at it. There I would read the date when Grandmother was born and when Grandfather was born and when they were married; when my parents were born and when their children were born.

Those records were interesting, but God keeps a more complete record than that. God kept your record before you married. God did not just keep the date of your birth and your marriage. He has kept it all. He has kept a record of your sins. God knows what kind of man you were before you married. God knows whether you left a slimy trail behind you or not. God knows! God knows the kind of woman you have been. As I have gone up and down this country I have had some shocking experiences. Oh, the women in this world whom you would never suspect, women who back in their girlhood days locked up skeletons in their hearts and threw the key away and have gone down life's way, hoping the key would never be found—always afraid of their record! God knows what kind of girl you were.

A girl said to me not long ago: "Oh, Dr. Jones, if I could just forget the past! If I could only forget! If I could only forget!"

One night in a southern city, after I dismissed a crowd and went to my room, somebody knocked at the door. I said, "Who is it?"

A voice said, "I want to talk to you about my soul." (I have never been too tired to answer that call.) There stood at the door a man. He walked into my room and said, "Bob Jones, there is one thing in my life I would give my right arm to forget. One thing—if I could just forget it! I can't forget it!" Yes, most of us have things we would like to forget.

A few years ago in New York City a woman came to my meeting at Calvary Baptist Church. She said to me, "I am haunted with a memory. I was a very wicked girl, a girl hard to control. Mother was a widow, an invalid. She had a hard time. I wanted to be going somewhere all the time. I neglected her. One day I said, 'Mother, may I do so-and-so?'

"She said, 'Darling, I don't want you to do that. Please, Mother doesn't want you to live that kind of life. It is not right; don't go to that place.' There she sat in an armchair. I went into a rage and fussed at my mother—just kept fussing. After a while she closed her eyes. I had seen her do that many times, and I thought she was praying; she always prayed when she did that. But I just kept on fussing. A few minutes later I spoke to her and she did not answer. I laid my hand on her and she was dead. She died while I was fussing at her. I just can't forget it!"

Oh, the things we would like to forget! I suppose all of us have something we want to forget, somebody we have caused some sorrow or pain, maybe somebody's heart we broke. Maybe it was a mother's or father's heart we broke—or some other sin we have committed.

God has kept your record. He has kept your record since you married. He knows the kind of husband you have been. He knows how many of those wrinkles you have pinched in the face of your wife. He knows how many gray hairs you have put in her head. He knows how many times you have made her pulse skip a beat and how many times she has gone to bed with a breaking heart and aching head because of you and your cruelty. He has kept your record. Through all these years God has been keeping the record. Talk about family skeletons! Talk about skeletons in the closet! You cannot keep them in the closet. You can lock them up, but sooner or later skeletons break down the closet door, go in the parlor and dance on the parlor floor. Then sometimes they walk down the front steps, go uptown and tell the world where they came from. But even if they do not break out of the closet now, some day millions and millions of family skeletons will be dangled in the faces of the teeming millions who stand before the judgment bar of God. The family record!

It Was a Rich Family

Now Jesus tells a story here. He says there was a rich man living in a certain community. He begins by telling us that he had plenty of money. A great many people think that is all they need, just money, money, money. Oh, the love of money! I never have understood how people love money. It looks to me as though the more they get, the more wretched they are, the more unhappy they are. I am not sorry for people who do not have much. I am sorry for folks who have a good deal. I spoke at the noon service today about the rich fool. You know when he got through, he went home and sat on the front porch and worried. He said to himself, 'Where shall I put my grain? What shall I do about a barn?' The men who had been working for him probably went home and went to sleep. Oh, the worry money brings!

This man had his money. He might have lived longer if he had not been rich. Maybe he ate too much. Or maybe he killed himself trying to get more money, grabbing for it. He was a rich man, clothed in purple and fine linen, living in luxury and wealth, having big parties all the time. Oh, the parties rich people have!

When I was in Rome a few years ago my guide said, "Doctor, look over yonder. That is where Roman society used to gather." They would get in there and eat and drink all they could, then they would tickle their throats with a feather and disgorge, and then start over again. After they would fill up that time, they would tickle their throat again, disgorge and start over. Day in and day out, a round of pleasure! Oh, what animal life! But you have folks like that now. There are people in this country living like that. I said to Mrs. Jones the other day, "Did you notice that nearly every woman who comes down the elevator with us in our hotel is bloated around the eyes?" Nearly every woman I see in the elevators of hotels look that way; they look dissipated. They do not look rested. We Christian people do not know what we really have in Jesus Christ. We do not realize how restful and sweet and blessed it is to be a Christian.

Now these folks had plenty of money. I imagine if your daughter had married into this family you would have said that she did well. I asked somebody the other day, "Is So-and-So married?"

"Oh, yes," somebody answered, "she did very well; she married a rich man." Oh, how foolish we are when we think that if we just had plenty of money we would be all right. These folks had plenty of money. They were a rich family.

It Was a Big Family

Now notice next that it was a big family. There were six brothers—one dead and five living. I do not know whether there were any girls or not. They did not count girls much in those days. Listen to me, woman: I do not see how a woman can reject Jesus Christ. The best Friend you ever had is Jesus. How any woman who knows that God loves her and Jesus died for her can reject Jesus is more than I can understand. I can understand how a coarse, ordinary, everyday, common man, with a man's body and a man's soul, might be mean enough to reject Jesus. But I cannot understand how a woman can do it—a woman, with a woman's soul, a woman's heart, a woman's emotions, a woman's responsiveness to kindness and love. In the name of common sense, how can any woman reject Jesus Christ!

Now, here they were—six brothers. That is a big family. Oh, those old big families! I was one of twelve children. If my mother and father had stopped with ten there would have been no preacher in the family. I am the eleventh. I am glad I grew up in a big family; I love big families. But rich families and big families do not usually go together. Rich folks have prosperity and the poor folks have posterity. But this family had riches and a big family, too. Six boys! I remember when I was a boy around the big open fireplace. Say, you can't make love around a radiator! Listen, you young fellows, if you have never had a country girl in front of an open fireplace, with a great big fire, and with roses in her cheeks—not artifical roses but real roses—and the luster of health in her eyes, you just don't know anything about a lovely picture! What a time we used to have around the fireside at night, father and mother and all the children; we were all trying to talk at one time, except my old daddy who would be trying to read. After a while he would say, "For goodness sake, get quiet; who can read around here?" But you couldn't keep them quiet. What fun we had! We could play all the games. We had enough for a ball team. We did not have to ask the neighbors in. The girls could play as well as the boys, and what fun we had. In the summertime we would sit under the stars at night and visit together and enjoy each other's company. We were not running to picture shows and always looking for excitement. We had each other and God and Christian faith and a happy home.

This was a big family. Don't you love children? Oh, I love little babies. The sweetest music the world has ever heard since morning stars sang together is the laughter of little babies. My son was here last night. He is thirty-four years old. If I could just turn back the clock of time and have him a wee little tot again! If I could hear him laugh once more! How quickly they get older. Then they grow up. The home gets broken and separation comes. Sometimes there is sin and sorrow. Oh, isn't the Devil mean? Isn't he mean to make homes wretched? And that is what he has done for some homes represented here tonight.

Here are a man and woman who started out in life together.

They loved each other. They stood at the altar and pledged their love until death did them part. Then the Devil came in between them. Then the son went astray after a while and broke the mother's heart, and the daughter went astray. Oh, how they have suffered. How homes have to suffer! How mothers and fathers grieve! But isn't it wonderful to have a family where everybody loves everybody else, where everybody is a Christian, and where all live in sweet fellowship?

A Family Visited by Death!

Now, here they are: a rich family, a big family; but a family that death has visited. One day one of the boys died. A hearse is backed up to the door. A piece of crepe is on the doorknob. The common people pass and say, "I wonder which one of the boys died?"

"Oh, he died, did he?"

"Yes, he died." Death. Death! Death is a wicked king. He is a cruel conqueror. His palace is a sepulcher. His pleasure fountains are filled with the tears of a weeping world, his music is the cry of broken hearts, and his flowers are the faded garlands on coffin lids. I hate death. There has never been anything beautiful about death to me. Don't try to make it beautiful. Death is not beautiful. It is the wages of sin. I hate it! I do not want to die. I want Jesus Christ to come. I do not want my loved ones to die. I do not like coffins and shrouds and tombstones and graveyards. Death is a horrible thing. But if Jesus tarries, you will be going pretty soon. Some of us haven't much longer. The wise man always makes preparation for the inevitable. Let me say that again. I want it to stay with you. The wise man always makes preparation for the inevitable. Death is the inevitable, and Jesus Christ is the preparation. You are a fool to live without Him. You do not have to do it. You do not have to go unprepared. You are a fool to go on rejecting Jesus Christ. Down the road there is a grave, a coffin, a shroud, a tombstone. Down the road is a monster, your enemy, the enemy of Jesus Christ, the last enemy to be destroyed. His name is death. He is going to come out of the bushes and put his fingers on your throat. You must meet him. Are you ready to die? Are you saved? Have you been born again?

I think I am about as game as the average man. I have been accused of a great many things in my life, but I do not believe anybody ever called me a coward. I have never been accused of running. But I would be afraid to be a sinner. I would not sleep until six o'clock tomorrow morning knowing what I know about saving grace, knowing that God loved me and Jesus died for me, knowing what I know about the Bible— I would not sleep until six o'clock tomorrow unsaved for all the money in the world. I might wake up in the morning rich, but I might wake up in Hell. You are crazy to go on without God. You are just crazy! You just do not show good sense. Listen! If the fire insurance policy on your house had expired today you could not sleep tonight. And yet you go to bed undisturbed, unafraid, not even thinking, with no insurance for your soul against the fires of Hell and the wrath of God. It is awful to be a sinner! It is terrible to be lost! And you do not have to be lost. There is no excuse for it. God Almighty wants to save you and Jesus loved you so much He went to Calvary and died to save you. Yet you are going on without God.

I remember one night in New York City I walked out of a mission and someone was passing out cards. This is what it said on those cards: "If I were to die tonight I would go to ———." Right under that it said, "Fill in and sign your name." I took that card and looked at it. It had a strange effect on me.

I was told about a drunken sailor who got one of those cards one time. He got on his boat and started to bed. Then he took the card out and looked at it. It said, "If I were to die tonight I would go to ———." He said, "Well, I know where I would go."

Listen, every sinner in this house knows you ought to go to Hell. "Oh," you say, "I am as good as anybody else." Listen, you know better than that! All that talk about how good you are—you know better than that. Don't talk to me like that. You know you do not deserve to go to Heaven. You know you are a sinner without God and you know you could not afford to meet your sins at the judgment.

That sailor got down on his knees and said, "My mother is a Christian. She taught me about God. She taught me about Jesus." He trusted Christ as his Saviour, got up and filled it in like this: "If I were to die tonight I would go to Heaven." Where would you go if you were to die tonight? As far as I know I am in perfect health. I went through a clinic recently and the doctor said my health was perfect, that my blood pressure was 120 and that I had the most perfect heart of any man my age he had ever known. But you know, I have known of doctors telling other people that and some of them died pretty soon afterwards. I am not a fool. I may die tonight. Some day I am going to preach my last sermon. This may be it. But if I die tonight I know exactly where I am going. If I did not know, I would not go to bed until I settled it. Listen, sinner, you do not have to go on in your sin. You can be saved before leaving this building.

The rich man died and was buried.

A Family with One Member in Hell

This was a rich family, a big family, a family with one member dead. Now I hate to say this next thing. It makes me shudder: It was a family with one member in Hell. I did not say that; Jesus said it, Jesus, the tender, loving, refined, gracious, kind Son of God. Nobody was ever so gentle, nobody ever so tender as Jesus Christ. Yet He said it. He said, "The rich man also died, and was buried; and in hell he lift up his eyes, being in torments" (Luke 16: 22, 23).

When Jesus preached a funeral He told things just as they

were. There was no cover-up process with Him. He said, 'This man died and was buried and went to Hell.' A member of the family is in Hell.

Some time ago I talked to a lovely, sweet woman. Her son had been killed in an automobile accident. He was a bad boy, so everybody said. That woman spent two or three hours trying to get me to say that I thought the boy might be in Heaven. I did not know what to say. I did not want to hurt her. She said, "You know, he asked me one day to pray for him." She went back to his babyhood and recalled the things he had said and every little thing that would give her hope. Then she said, "Do you suppose, Brother Jones, my boy is in Heaven?"

"Well," I said, "If he trusted Jesus [maybe he did; I do not know] he is in Heaven." Oh, a loved one in Hell! A loved one to die without God and without hope! To follow that one to the cemetery, knowing, according to the Word of God, that he is lost!

Now, let me tell you something: tonight you have a loved one. You had better get him saved. Somebody here tonight has a loved one unsaved. You had better bring him to this meeting. You had better get him in these services. You had better get him to Jesus Christ. You had better do it before it is too late! Now is the time! "Now is the day of salvation."

Years ago I was in a meeting in Knoxville, Tennessee, in George R. Stuart's church. One day Dr. Stuart and I were out driving. We passed a home and Dr. Stuart said, "Bob, the finest official member of my church lives in that home. He is the loveliest man I think I ever knew. And he has the sweetest wife. They did not have any children and they kept praying for God to send a baby to their home. One day they said, 'Well, we are going down to the orphans' home and get us a baby. We are going to adopt a baby; we've just got to have a baby.'

"One day God sent them a little baby all their own. He was the sweetest baby boy you ever saw. He grew up to be about four or five years old. He was such an attractive, magnetic little fellow. His father would bring him to town and if he introduced him to somebody he would shake hands and say, 'I'm happy to meet you.'

"The father would come home at night, stop the car at the garage door, blow his horn; the little boy would run out, open the door, get in the car and ride on in with his father. Then he would climb up into his father's arms and his father would bring him into the house.

"A few nights ago the father drove in, stopped outside, blew the horn and nobody answered. He blew it again and nobody answered. Then the father got out, opened the garage door, got back in the car and started to drive into the garage. Just as he did so the little boy jumped out and said, 'Boo, Daddy!' The automobile ran over him. The father pulled him out from between the wheels and took him up into his arms. The little fellow tried to smile. He kissed his daddy in the mouth and laid his head on his father's shoulder. The father took him in the house and put him on the bed and he was dead.

"I never saw a funeral like it in my life. That man—the great big, wonderful man that he was—got down on his knees, put his arms around that little casket, lifted it clear up and said, 'Daddy didn't mean to do it. You know Daddy wouldn't have done that to you. Daddy loves you. You know Daddy wouldn't have done his baby boy like that.' "

Dr. Stuart sat there as he told me the story and just cried. And I cried, too. Then he said to me, "Bob, isn't that the saddest thing you ever heard?"

I said, "Doctor, there are worse things in Knoxville than that."

He said, "What do you mean?"

I said, "In the city of Knoxville there are mothers and fathers into whose arms God has put helpless little babies. God said, 'Bring them up for Me.' And they have been careless and sinful. They have let those children go out into eternity lost." Listen! It is not as bad to run an automobile over a little boy as it is for a parent to run the car of evil influence over a child and send his soul to Hell.

Somebody in Hell! A member of the family damned because you did not do anything about it, because you did not care. Now listen to me, you Christians; we are so careless, so neglectful! We neglect the important things, the big things, and wreck our children's lives and the lives of our loved ones, the lives of our brothers and sisters and neighbors and friends.

A Family with Five Others on the Way to Hell!

Notice the next step in the family—a rich family, a big family, a family with a member in Hell, and a family with five others on their way to Hell. Now, I did not say that. The rich man in Hell said, "I pray thee therefore, father, that thou wouldest send him to my father's house: For I have five brethren; that he may testify unto them, lest they also come into this place of torment" (Luke 16:27, 28). He was saying, 'Abraham, send Lazarus back and ask my brothers not to come here. I have five brothers on their way here and I do not want them to come.'

I suppose it is awfully human, but I have always thought that having the whole family in Heaven would make Heaven sweeter. Maybe I should not say that, but I have always felt that way. I remember when I was a boy in the country—my father was a Methodist and my mother was a Baptist—we used to entertain the Baptist conventions and the Methodist conferences. Oh, the company we had in those days! We did not think anything about having company when I was boy. I slept in the cotton house nearly every Saturday night until I was almost grown.

And I remember on Sunday when we used to have company we would fill that great big table, then fill it again, and still again. Late in the afternoon the company would begin to leave and then my sisters' beaus would begin to come, some of them on horseback and some of them in buggies. They would drive up to that country home.

And here is the strange thing about it: about that time my father would get down an old hickory stick he brought home from the battlefield of Chickamauga where he was wounded. My father and mother seemed to understand each other; they did not have to talk. He would just get that old stick and my mother understood that he was going over to the cemetery. I had two sisters buried there. My father would lead the way. My mother would follow. And my little brother younger than myself and I used to go with them, down a little path through the field, and over a foot log across the stream—not around the road, that was too far. We would stop on our way and get water out of the stream and gather magnolias and wild honeysuckles (that is my favorite flower). Then we would go on to the graves. My father and mother would stand by the graves. My mother would fix the flowers while my father leaned on his stick. My father did not say anything. Mother always cried. She would water those flowers with her tears. After they got through—you know it seems strange as I think about it now: my father did not say, "Well, we'd better go." They just seemed to understand each other. He led the way and she went along, then my brother went next, and I came last.

Then one day my mother died. My father, my little brother and I used to go and put flowers on her grave. Then my father always cried.

Then one day my father died. Then my brother died. They are all gone but me. Two weeks ago I buried the last sister. I am the only one of twelve children that is left. I get a little lonely sometimes. I did not really know how lonely it would be to be the only one of the family left. If the Lord tarries I will be going myself some time. But I have it all worked out: when I get to Heaven I am going to ask Jesus for a special favor. I am going to ask Him to let me and my folks get off to ourselves once in a while. I do not want any company. I do not want any visitors. I just want my family: my mother and father and my sisters and brothers. I want us to sit down and just talk things over, and I do not want to miss any of them. It would not seem exactly right if everybody was not there. Did you ever have a family reunion when they were not all there? It did not seem right, did it?

You know, I think Heaven is going to be more real than we ever dreamed it would be. Heaven seems to be more real to my friends who have grown old and who have been Christians for years. It is more real to me than it used to be.

A Family Which Had Every Needed Chance to Be Saved

Here was a big family, a rich family, one of them dead, one of them in Hell, five others on the way. And now one last word. It was a family that had every chance it needed to be saved. That man did not have to go to Hell. His five brothers did not have to go. They had Moses and the prophets. They had a testimony. They could have been saved. But listen! You are this side of Calvary. You are this side of the open tomb. You have a chance greater than they had. You have the gospel. You are in the Holy Ghost dispensation. You are in the church age. You are in the gathering-out period, when God is getting a bride for His Son. You have a chance. If you never had one before tonight, you have this one tonight. If you never hear the gospel again, you are hearing it now. If you never have another call, you have a call tonight. Why don't you settle it tonight? Do not go out of this house without settling it; please do not. Let me beg you to settle it. I want to do you a favor. I want you to be saved. It is wonderful to be saved! You feel so safe when you are saved. You can go to bed at night and rest in peace. Won't you come to God tonight? Won't you trust Jesus? Don't lose this chance. Now is your chance. Your last chance will come some day; this may be it. Don't let it pass! Trust Him tonight!

Chapter 8

THE MIRACLE OF CALVARY

"And when they were come to the place, which is called Calvary, there they crucified him, and the malefactors, one on the right hand, and the other on the left. Then said Jesus, Father, forgive them; for they know not what they do. And they parted his raiment, and cast lots. And the people stood beholding. And the rulers also with them derided him, saying, He saved others; let him save himself, if he be Christ, the chosen of God. And the soldiers also mocked him, coming to him, and offering him vinegar, And saying, If thou be the king of the Jews, save thyself. And a superscription also was written over him in letters of Greek, and Latin, and Hebrew, THIS IS THE KING OF THE JEWS. And one of the malefactors which were hanged railed on him saying, If thou be Christ, save thyself and us. But the other answering rebuked him, saying, Dost not thou fear God, seeing thou art in the same condemnation? And we indeed justly; for we receive the due reward of our deeds: but this man hath done nothing amiss. And he said unto Jesus, Lord, remember me when thou comest into thy kingdom. And Jesus said unto him, Verily I say unto thee, To day shalt thou be with me in paradise."
—Luke 23:33–43.

I CALL YOUR attention to all these verses but especially to these two: "And he said unto Jesus, Lord, remember me when thou comest into thy kingdom. And Jesus said unto him, Verily I say unto thee, To day shalt thou be with me in paradise."

When Jesus Christ was in this world a man came to Him one day and said, "Good Master."

Jesus asked, 'Why do you call Me good? There is only One who is good and that is God.' In other words, Jesus said, 'If

145

I am not God, I am not good.' If Jesus was not God, He was not good. If He was not God, He was the greatest impostor the world ever knew. He was either God or a terrible blasphemer.

Now, He *was* God. I know He was God. Nobody but God could do for me what Jesus Christ did when He saved me. I did not need any theologian to tell me I had met God when I was saved. I knew I had met God. Any sinner who has met Jesus Christ, and trusted Him for salvation, knows He has met God. He may not understand some things, but the man who doubts the deity of Jesus Christ has never been born again. You can put that down in your book and let it stay there. The man who questions the deity of Jesus Christ does not know Jesus Christ, and the man who denies His deity has never been born again. People tell us this is a scientific age. They say, "Let's make experiments." All right, if you wonder who Jesus is, why don't you make an experiment? Turn yourself over to Him and you can find out who He is. He is none other than the Son of God.

Jesus, a Miracle-Worker

Now, since He was God it is not surprising that He had power to do everything He did. There were many things in His life which took place in a rather strange way. His birth was strange and the lowly place He held in a manger. It was strange how Jesus Christ, a little baby, was God manifest in the flesh. It was strange how He sat in the temple as a youth at the age of twelve talking to doctors of the law. It was strange about His baptism in Jordan. It was strange just how the Devil came to Him in the wilderness, on the mountaintop, and on the pinnacle of the temple. It was strange how with wonderful simplicity the God of this universe, manifest in human flesh, went about making the blind to see, the deaf to hear, the dumb to speak; curing the palsied, cleansing the leper and raising the dead. And, young people, let me tell you this in passing: simplicity is truth's most becoming garb.

Do not ever get beyond the simple. Yes, it was wonderful how He did all of these things. But, men and women, to my mind, the strangest thing that Jesus Christ ever did was when He hung in the darkness that clustered about Golgotha and said to a dying man, "To day shalt thou be with me in paradise."

Now you talk to me about miracles, if Jesus did what He said He did—and I do not say *if* with any question in my mind—if Jesus Christ at Calvary could take this man who was fit for Hell and in a moment of time make him a fit subject for Heaven, Jesus Christ could perform any miracle recorded in the New Testament. Talk about miracles! The most marvelous miracle of which I can conceive is the miracle of regenerating grace in a human heart, the miracle of Jesus Christ's taking a poor, miserable, Hell-bound sinner and in a second of time fixing him up so he is fit to walk streets of gold under a cloudless sky and keep company with God and the angels in Heaven forever! That is more wonderful than raising the dead. I read in the Bible about Jesus going to a home where there was a dead girl. He said, 'She is not dead but asleep.' He touched her and brought her to life. I say, "That is wonderful!" But it is not so wonderful as this. I read about that funeral procession going down the street—and Jesus always sees funeral processions. There is not any sorrow He does not feel. No tear of sorrow ever flows down a human cheek that He does not feel on His own. He sees all the funeral processions, all the pinched and hungry faces of little children, and all the sobbing hearts of men and women everywhere. So the funeral procession moved along. Jesus went up and touched the bier, and there sprang from that bier the comfort of a mother's heart. Oh, how wonderful that was! But here He is at Calvary with nails in His hands and a spike through His feet. He is hanging there in seeming helplessness and yet as He hangs He turns and says to a man who is not fit to live on earth, 'Never mind, you are good enough to go to paradise with Me.' That is a miracle. That is more wonderful than bringing a widow's son back from the bier.

I read about His going to the tomb of Lazarus. Lazarus had been dead four days. Decomposition had already set in. The sisters shrank from the decomposed body in the open sepulcher. He said, "Lazarus, come forth." And there walked from that grave the brother of Mary and Martha. I say, "Wonderful miracle!" It was, but oh, men and women, He is doing something at Calvary more wonderful than that. Here is a man who for years has been dead in trespasses and sin, a man helplessly enslaved, a man who can do nothing for himself, a man whose only claim on Jesus is the claim of his sins; and Jesus is bearing that in His own body. And He faces that poor, lost, sinful, dead, hopeless, helpless man and says, 'You are good enough to live with Me in paradise.' That is more wonderful than raising Lazarus from the dead.

Listen! Some things that have happened in this building the last few days are as wonderful as any miracle recorded in the New Testament. I remember the other night a man walked up to the front and said to me, "About thirty years ago in Mansfield, Ohio, I found God. I found Jesus Christ. I was a poor sinner. I have been in China for twenty years as a missionary." He was a man who had never dreamed of being a missionary, and yet God saved him and so made him over that he said, "It is China for me."

A night or two later another man walked up to me and said, "Twenty-five years ago in Grand Rapids one night after church you led me to Jesus Christ. You got down and prayed for me and I was saved. I got on the train and came to Chicago and begged them to take me into Moody Bible Institute. They did. And now for over twenty years I have been in Manila, over in the Philippine Islands all these years. For three long years I was in a Japanese prison." Say, who could do that for men except Jesus? Who but Jesus! Who but the Son of God could do that for people? What a wonderful Saviour is Jesus! Oh, the miracles He performs!

Some years ago I was in Cleveland, Ohio. One night I was sitting in my room just before church and a man knocked at the door. I went to the door and there was a handsome gentleman. He said, "I want to talk to you just a minute. My name is So-and-So. Years ago as a miserable, drunken bum I went down the street in Mansfield, Ohio. I saw a big sign out in front of the building which said, 'Bob Jones Tabernacle,' and I dropped in there and sat down near a furnace. I got warm and dropped off to sleep. After a while I waked up and the building was crowded. I was in almost a stupor. I hardly knew where I was. But you were up there saying, 'Jesus can save you. You may have broken every commandment, but Jesus can save. You may be enslaved by sin and passion and habit, but Jesus can save you.'

"I wondered if that were so. And I, the poor, miserable bum that I was, staggered down to the front and found Jesus. I went through World War I and became a chaplain. Now I am back here at home with a sales organization of several hundred men." And I think he said he had led three hundred of them to Jesus Christ.

Say, who said that Jesus Christ has quit performing miracles?

Years ago in Grand Rapids Mel Trotter showed me all of those hypodermic needles which had been used by men enslaved by the dope habit until saved in the Mel Trotter Mission, and told me the story of what God had done through that mission. Say, listen! Jesus Christ has not gone out of business. He is the same yesterday, today, and forever; and He is performing miracles around the world. He has performed miracles in some of our lives.

Some years ago in New York one Friday night they said to me, "Say, Dr. Jones, how about coming down to the mission on the Bowery, the Jerry McAuley Mission? It is free-supper night and there will be a lot of bums there. How about coming?"

I said, "All right; I'll do it." So I went down there. There were two or three hundred men in attendance. Up in the front were men of priestly bearing. Back in the rear there were

the bumiest of the bums and the slimiest of the slums and the
toughest of the tough. We sang some songs and had prayer
and read the Word. Then I made a talk, and had a testimony
meeting. A man got up. I think he was the handsomest man
I ever saw. As I remember it, this is what he said: "Years ago
I staggered into this building the most hopeless bum that ever
came in here. There is not a man here tonight like me. I was
in a worse fix than any of you, boys. I was reared out West
and graduated from university with a degree in law. I married
my boyhood sweetheart and we started out in life. My father
gave me a check for $100,000 and my share of the estate. My
wife and I got into society and began to live a worldly life. I
became dissipated and wretched. I spent all of my fortune and
got rid of all I had. One day my wife had to go back home with
our baby to get something to eat and some clothes. I took to
the highway and traveled all over this country. Finally I
came to New York. I was a helpless wreck and was in the
hospital five times with delirium tremens. I could not quit
drinking. I did not want to drink. I loved my wife and baby,
but I was a slave, a hopeless slave. At last I went to a friend of
mine—I knew a little something about law—and played
crazy. They took me in the insane asylum for nine months.
I came out at the end of nine months and laughed at them and
said, 'I was not crazy; I came there to get away from drink.
I'm a free man now, and I'm going to get my wife and baby
back.' I came to New York City, and the first place I stopped
was a saloon. I slept on whisky barrels for over a month,
night after night, and swept out saloons for my drink. One
day, helpless and hopeless and ruined, I staggered into this
mission, knelt up there at the front, and God Almighty saved
me in a flash. I have never had a drop of whisky from that day
until this, and I'm here in New York doing well in business.
My wife is with me, and my baby girl is a young lady. They
are both Christians."

Say, who said Jesus Christ has quit the miracle business?
"Oh," but you say, "Bob Jones, we are not that kind of peo-

ple." Wait a minute. There are slaves in this house tonight. There are people in this building tonight—respectable people, supposedly decent, refined people—who are slaves to sin. You have said a thousand times, "I'll never do that again," and you did it again. And you said, "So help me, God, it's the last time I'll ever commit that sin," and you committed it within a week. Through the years it has been one promise after another made and broken, and you are held tonight in the chains of habit and sin. Respectable people! O God, be merciful to respectable sinners! You said, "Never again, never again," but it was over and over and over. Do you know what you need? You need a miracle in your life. You need somebody who can set you free. "Oh," but you say, "Bob Jones, you don't know me. I was born wrong." Oh, but bless God, you can be born right. God Almighty helps folks start over again. "Oh," but you say, "I've got the devils in me— demons!" Yes, but Jesus Christ is able to cast out those demons. He can set you free. That is what He did at the cross.

Now get the picture for just a moment. If there was ever a time when Jesus seemed helpless, it was on Calvary. There He hung on the cross. You know, I have always wanted to be an artist. There is one picture I have always wanted to put on canvas. If I could paint the picture of the cross with Jesus hanging on it as I have seen it with the eyes of my soul, I would get the heart of this world. I would paint a picture of the hands of Jesus. Did you ever stop to think about those hands—those hands that fondled the cheek of a mother; those hands that swept clouds out of human skies; those hands that touched blind, sightless eyes and made them see and deaf ears and made them hear; those hands that broke bread to feed the hungry? The last time the mortal eyes of men ever saw Jesus, His hands were stretched out in blessing. I would like to paint a picture of those hands—those hands that were torn by cruel nails for you and me.

Did you ever think about the feet of Jesus? Those feet that never made a selfish step; those feet that ever went on errands of mercy; those feet that were accustomed to royal carpets up in Heaven; those feet that were accustomed to the courts of the sky, came down to tread the dusty roads of earth. And those feet were torn by cruel nails for you and me.

Did you ever think about the heart of Jesus—that heart that was a stranger to selfishness and malice and strife; that heart that exclaimed those words of such matchless pathos, "And ye will not come to me, that ye might have life" (John 5:40). That heart broke one day for you and me. Say, do you love Jesus? I just do not see how anybody could keep from loving Him. You need not tell me that men are depraved. I need no other argument for total depravity than the argument that men in sin do not love Jesus. Listen, man, if you have a heart in your bosom, you will have to love Him. Woman, you listen to me! If there is a woman's soul in your body, you will have to love Jesus. The greatest moral monstrosity in the world is a woman who does not love Him. I just do not understand it. I wonder how anybody could keep from loving Him. Do not tell me that there is no Hell. Do not tell me that men are not sinners. If men were not sinners, all men would love Jesus. The one Person the whole world would love would be Jesus, if men were not sinners. Don't you love Him? If you do not love Him, you may know you are a sinner. I saw Him when I was a little child.

> I saw One hanging on the tree
>   In agony and blood,
> Who fixed His languid eye on me
>   As near the cross I stood.

And I have loved Him since that day. He is dearer to me than the memory of my precious mother, dearer to me than wife and son. I do not see how anybody could keep from loving Him. Do you love Him? Oh, sinner, poor sinner, if you would just trust Him and let Him save you, you would fall in love with Him. What a wonderful Saviour!

The Prayer of a Sinner

Now Jesus is on the cross there—get the picture—as this man prayed. Do you ever pray? Oh, I don't mean, Do you *say* prayers? There is too much prayer-saying and too little prayer-praying. We say prayers. But I am asking you tonight, Do you ever pray? You know, there is something of Calvary in prayer. There is something of blood and darkness and agony. There is a kind of soul-refreshing agony in prayer. There is something about prayer that gets mixed up with Calvary.

It is midnight, and the lights are out in most of the homes; but yonder across the street is a widow's cottage. The shades are drawn, but there are a few dim rays of light that get beyond the shade out into the street. I wonder what is there. There in that room, prostrate by the bed, with her face turned to Heaven, and with tears flowing down her cheeks, is that widowed mother. She is saying, "O God, I have a son somewhere. Oh, my poor boy, my lost boy, my boy out in sin! O God, my Father, please put about my boy Thine arms and bring him back." Say, that woman has some of Calvary in her prayer. Do you know what we need in this country? We need an old-time baptism of real crying unto God, agonizing prayer, prayer stained with Calvary's blood and baptized with Calvary's agony. This man prayed.

Now wait a minute—he prayed for himself. I do not want to shock you, but I want to say something which I want you to think through for just a minute. You know, I cannot find in the Bible anywhere that God ever told a sinner to pray to be saved. Now do not misunderstand me. I can find examples where sinners did pray and were saved, and I can find statements like, "Whosoever shall call on the name of the Lord shall be saved" (Acts 2:21). But nowhere in the Bible can I find that God ever told a sinner to pray to be saved. I can find where God tells a sinner to repent, tells a sinner to believe, tells a sinner to obey the gospel; but He does not tell sinners to pray to be saved. I got to wondering about it one day, and I think I understand it. You do not have to tell a sinner to pray to be saved. You cannot find in the Bible anywhere where God ever told a mother to love her baby. Doesn't God want mothers to love their babies? Why, certainly. Well, why doesn't He tell them to? He does not have to. You may not have wanted that little baby. You may have been selfish and wanted your own way and your own pleasure. But one day a little baby was laid in your arms. A little velvety hand got on your cheek, and a little baby's breath blew in your face. A little baby cried in your ear. God did not have to say, "Love that baby." Your mother heart began to hug it. Your mother heart said, "Yes, God. Yes, God."

And you know, if you could see Jesus dying for you, you would not have to be told to pray to be saved. If he sees Him on the cross, it is as natural for a sinner to cry out to Jesus as it is for mothers to love their babies. When I saw Him and knew He was dying for me, I could not help saying, "O Jesus, be merciful to me!" I thought about David when he wandered from God and came back and said, "Lord, restore unto me the joy of thy salvation" (Psa. 51:12). And I thought about the publican in the temple who was too humble to lift his guilty head but smote his breast and said, "God be merciful to me a sinner" (Luke 18:13).

Just before day, one morning years ago, a train pulled into the suburbs of a little town in the South and suddenly stopped. There was a traveling man aboard the Pullman, all dressed and ready to get off the train. He wondered why the sudden stop. After a while he went out on the platform and saw the door open. He stepped off on the ground and looked down the track. There was the conductor, the flagman, the fireman, the engineer, and the porters all gathered around. He went down there and said, "What's the matter?"

They said, "We've just run over this poor fellow. He was crossing the track, and the train cut off his limbs. We tied up the stubs the best we could, and maybe we can save him; but he looks awfully bad."

The conductor said, "I'll run over here and wake up this man and call for the ambulance. I'll be back in just a minute." He came back quickly and said, "The ambulance is coming."

The traveling man said to the porter, "Get my baggage off the train quickly." Then he said, "Captain, you can pull your train on in. My hotel is right near the hospital, and I'll get in and ride with this poor fellow."

By this time the train pulled out, and the ambulance came. They picked up the legless man and put him in the ambulance. They put his lower limbs in, too. And this traveling man, this stranger friend, climbed up with him; and they rode rapidly down the street. The moon was still shining in the sky, pouring pale light through the window into the pale face of the wounded, bleeding, weak man. The stars were still shining. Just about that time, before they reached the hospital, the man looked over and said, "My friend, will you pray for me?"

The man said, "I'm sorry pal. I'm awfully sorry, pal; but I don't know how to pray. I never have prayed in my life."

Then the wounded man said, "Say, pal, could you tell me a prayer I could pray? I want to pray, and I don't know how to pray."

"Well," he said, "I heard a prayer like this. I don't know whether it is any good or not. You might try it. 'God, be merciful to me a sinner.' You might just pray that prayer."

The wounded man said, "God, be merciful to me a sinner."

And the man said, "You know, I notice when I go to church the preacher always closes his prayer with the statement, 'For Jesus' sake. Amen.' You might try that. You might say, 'God, be merciful to me a sinner, for Jesus' sake. Amen.' I don't know why they do it that way, but that's the way the preacher, I notice, always closes his prayer."

The poor, weak man said, "God, be merciful to me a sinner, for Jesus' sake. Amen." Then he said, "That's a good prayer. I don't understand it, but it is not dark now. Something has happened. The load is all lifted. I have peace in my heart. I do not understand it, but say, why don't *you* pray that prayer? It is a good prayer. You might try it. It is a wonderful prayer. It does something for you." By the time they got to the hospital and took him upstairs and put him in the bed, he was dead.

Seeing such a change come over this dying man, and knowing something had happened beyond human understanding, this traveling man looked toward the eastern sky just as the morning was standing tiptoe on the horizon, turned his face up to the sky above him and said, "God, be merciful to me a sinner, for Jesus' sake. Amen." And he has been a Christian ever since.

O sinner, if you are here tonight, I want to tell you a wonderful story. Jesus Christ died on Calvary's cross so God could be merciful to all sinners, and there is mercy for you and salvation for you as there was mercy and salvation for this man.

The Tragedy of Sin

Let's turn the picture around quickly for a moment. I want to show you something that I did not see for years and that I would like for you to see tonight. At the beginning of the crucifixion, both of these thieves railed on Christ. (We do not get it here but from the other Gospels. Both of them railed on Jesus.) Now get the picture. Here are three crosses. Here is a cross in the center, and there is a Person hanging on that cross. He is always in the center. He is always the center—Jesus Christ is never anywhere else. And the mob is out there—the cursing, mocking, hissing mob. They are all talking to this One. And these two thieves at the beginning of the crucifixion, both of them, join with the mob in mocking Jesus. They say to Him, 'Yeah, You're the Son of God. Why don't You come down from the cross? You are the Son of God! Why don't You save Yourself and us, too?' Say, there is the worst picture of human depravity in all literature. Let us suppose that to begin with both of them thought Jesus Christ was a criminal like themselves. Let us suppose that they thought He was just a man like they were and that He deserved to die like they did. Let us *suppose* that. Wouldn't you have thought that they would have said a kind word to Him? It seems to me that they would have turned and said, "Never mind. Never mind what they say to you. Never mind, pal. Yes, you cowardly, cursing, mocking mob, it is easy enough to get somebody on the cross and make fun of him. But never mind, pal, don't pay any attention to them. We will take it like men. Never mind what they say to you." But they did not. They joined with a mocking, cursing, hissing mob and hurled into the teeth of their companion in death the mockery of the mob who nailed him to a cross. That is human depravity. Listen! That shows you what people will do when they begin to play with sin. That shows you the degrading, damning, blighting power of sin in a human life. O God, pity people who play with sin!

I remember one time years ago in Montgomery, Alabama, I walked down the street and met a man who had a sad face. He said, "Dr. Bob, isn't the governor of this state a friend of yours?"

I said, "Yes, sir, he's on the board of trustees at our college and my personal friend."

He said, "Will you do me a favor? My boy under twenty years of age is out at Kilby Prison and is to be electrocuted just after midnight. You have heard about it and read it in the papers. You are a father. Won't you go up to the capitol and ask Governor Graves to commute that sentence to life imprisonment?"

I said, "My friend, I would like to do that for you, but I would not presume to ask the governor to do that. Governor Graves is a lawyer; he is judicial; he has weighed all the evidence; he knows all the facts. You have asked him to set aside the verdict of the court and the verdict of the jurors, and if he has any way he can do it honorably, he will. I would never be presumptuous enough to ask that of my friend. I would not dare to do it because he is in a judicial position. I would not dare do it. I am awfully sorry. I would like to do it for you, but I cannot."

Then he looked at me and said, "Will you do me a favor?"

And I said, "I would do anything I could for you."

He said, "Will you go out to the prison and talk to my boy? The chaplain has talked to him, and my pastor has talked to him, but he will not even pray. I cannot let him die without praying."

I said, "Well, I wish I could do it, but I have a speaking engagement, and it will take all of my time to get there. I wish I could, but I just can't. But I know the chaplain well, and he is a wonderful man. He knows more about how to do that than anybody else I know, and if he can't, there is nothing I could do. But I will pray for him."

He said, "All right."

So we got in the car and drove on down to my speaking engagement that night. After the service we started back to the city, and I said to Mrs. Jones and the friends in the car, "I am going out to Kilby Prison and see that boy."

Mrs. Jones said, "I wouldn't go. When you go with those boys to the chair, you die with them, and you have all you can live under. The strain is more than you can stand. I wouldn't go."

"But," I said, "I have a boy; I'm going. I would never feel right if I didn't go."

We got out there and parked our car just before midnight. Just as I was parking my car the death wagon drove up. Oh, it was a morbid sort of thing! There was the boy, only twenty years of age, and the death wagon out there waiting. I went in the prison. I knew the warden. He said, "That is all right, Dr. Bob; go right ahead." I went down the corridor and on down to death row, and up to the cell where the boy was. His hair was all shaved. Nobody was near him. The chaplain was standing over to one side crying.

I walked up to the cell door and said, "My name is Bob Jones. I saw your father and he asked me to come and talk to you."

He said, "I wish you preachers would let me alone. I asked the chaplain to go away and not hound me. I am going to die like a man. I am not going to be a baby and ask God to do anything for me. Do not ask me to pray. I am going to walk to that chair and sit down and die like a man. I'm not going to be a coward and a baby and a weakling—not me."

I stood there and tried to talk to him, and he almost pushed me from the cell door. I went over to the chaplain, and the chaplain said to me under his breath, "He is the only criminal in this prison that I have ever felt as I do about. I think he ought to die."

Listen! He wasn't brave. He wasn't a hero. That is not courage. That is not manhood. That is not backbone. That is not fortitude. That is rotten, hellish depravity. That shows you what sin can do for a man before he is twenty years old.

Oh, we wonder about the atrocious crimes being committed. You wonder about the young people of today and say, "Oh, how can they do what they do?" They can do it because sin has right of way. And you do not know where you are going when you go to playing with sin.

I was in a campaign in Texas years ago. One night during that campaign I walked down the street with a prominent Christian layman. He said to me, "Say, Dr. Jones, have you read in the paper about Rev. ———, that preacher in Boston who is charged with the murder of that woman?"

I said, "Yes, I read about it."

He said, "What do you think about it?"

I said, "Well, I can't tell much about it because we just do not know the truth about it from reading the papers."

He said, "Well, I know."

I said, "You know what?"

He said, "He is innocent. If they put that man in the chair they are going to railroad an innocent man. He used to be my pastor. I have heard him preach many a time. He was not a murderer; that man was not that kind. I do not think he was a strong character. I always thought he had some weaknesses, but he could not kill anybody. He was the most harmless character I ever knew. And they are just railroading him to the chair. I believe they are going to put him there. And if they do, they are going to put an innocent man there as sure as the world."

The next morning I bought a paper in the hotel lobby and read in big headlines across the front page where, "Rev. ———— in his Boston cell said, 'I killed that woman.' "

I went across the lobby and said, "Did you read this?"

He answered, "Oh, yes; I read it." Then he said, "O my Lord, how could he do it? How could he do it? I have sat under his preaching. I was a deacon in his church. I heard him many times. He has been to my home. He has had family prayer with me. How could he do it! How could he do it! I do not understand." After a little he said, "I couldn't do that, could you, Bob Jones? Could you kill a woman like that?"

I said, "You do not know what you could do."

He asked, "What do you mean?"

I said, "Two years ago this morning Rev.—perhaps would have thrown up his hands in horror as you are doing. But he began to play with sin. He won the heart of a girl. He wormed his way into her soul. He plucked from her brow the diadem of her purity. He plucked the roses of decency and modesty from her cheeks and threw them away. He sacrificed her on the altar of his lust. And after he did that he became so hardened that he then stained his hands with the lifeblood of the woman he ruined. No man knows where he will go when he begins to play with sin." I am afraid of sin! All my life I have been afraid of sin. That is the only thing I am afraid of. I think I can say what few men have ever said. Maybe I am a fool but I have never had much sense of physical fear. I do not know much about it. But I have always been afraid of sin. God saved me when I was eleven years old. I am now sixty-two. He has kept me from tragedy and disgrace. I am afraid of sin. I have always been afraid of sin. I never hear of some preacher falling that I do not say, "O God, help me." I never hear of a Christian worker dishonoring the name of Jesus that I do not say, "O God, let me die, let me die before anything happens to me." Oh, you young people and you Christian workers, listen to me! The shores of time are strewn with the wrecks of Christian workers who played with sin. Watch your step! WATCH YOUR STEP! Take care! Beware! Do not play with sin! If you want people to think you are brave, let me tell you what to do. Go out in the mountains of the West, find a nest of rattlesnakes and take them up in your arms and play with them. Take them to bed with you. If you want people to think you are brave, go down to the powerhouse and play with a few thousand volts of electricity. If you want people to think you are a hero, climb up into the clouds, get into the dark pavilion of a storm and play with forked lightning. But do not act the fool; do not play with sin!

The Grace of God

But wait a minute! Sin never took a man so low but that the arm of God's grace could reach a little lower. As low as sin dragged this thief, the arm of God's grace reached down and picked him up. Men may have said, "You are not good enough to live with us. We are going to put you on a cross and end you."

Jesus said, "I'll fix you so you will be good enough to live with Me." One morning he was drinking the vinegar and the gall and before evening came he drank from the fountain that flowed from the throne.

Years ago in one of our American cities a son of one of the most princely leaders died. The father was brokenhearted. He went from bad to worse, and from worse to still worse. And one night, coatless and hatless and shoeless, he staggered into a mission where he had heard a bum, a hungry bum, could get a sandwich and a cup of coffee. He took his seat in the back of the building with the bums. The leader of the service said, "Boys, is there anybody here who can play the piano? Our pianist did not come tonight. Can any of you fellows play for me?"

Everything was still for a minute and then the coatless, hatless, shoeless, bleary-eyed, bloated-faced bum got up and came staggering and trembling down the aisle. He said, "Mister, when I was a boy I took some piano lessons. I haven't played for years. You notice I'm in an awful bad fix. My nerves are shot to pieces. I do not know whether I can do it or not. But if you can't get anybody else and are willing to try me, I will see what I can do for you."

The leader said, "Sit down there." Then he opened the book to a song about the blood and he talked about the blood of Christ a little while. He told how Jesus died on the cross, how He shed His blood to wash away sin, how He could save anybody. Then he read a verse of the song and looked around at the pianist. He was sitting there trembling, stooped under the weight of his dissipation and sin, and he said, "All right, you may start now."

The man looked at his book a minute. He was a little hesitant. Then he straightened up the best he could and started to play. The old skill came back and before he played the first stanza through he had played himself into the arms of God. That is just like Jesus!

> There is a fountain filled with blood
> 　Drawn from Immanuel's veins;
> And sinners, plunged beneath that flood,
> 　Lose all their guilty stains.
>
> The dying thief rejoiced to see
> 　That fountain in his day;
> And there may I, though vile as he,
> 　Wash all my sins away.
>
> Dear dying Lamb, Thy precious blood
> 　Shall never lose its power,

Till all the ransomed Church of God
  Be saved, to sin no more.

E'er since, by faith, I saw the stream
  Thy flowing wounds supply,
Redeeming love has been my theme,
  And shall be till I die.

Then in a nobler, sweeter song,
  I'll sing Thy power to save,
When this poor lisping, stammering tongue
  Lies silent in the grave.

Sinner, if you are here tonight and are able to run, run to Jesus. But if you are too weak and sin-sick to run, walk up to Calvary. If you are too weak, just stand up and look in that direction. If you are so far gone that you cannot stand up, just turn your face that way. If you are too weak for that, just open your eyes and look, for there is life for a look at the crucified One. But if you are so far gone and so weak and so sick that you cannot open your eyes, then when your heart beats, let the grace of God slip in. You may have come in here tonight a hopeless lost man or woman; but you can walk out of that door tonight good enough to live in Heaven forever. What a wonderful Saviour is Jesus!

Chapter 9

JESUS—THE LIGHT OF THE WORLD

"Then spake Jesus again unto them, saying, I am the light of the world: he that followeth me shall not walk in darkness, but shall have the light of life."—John 8:12.

"Ye are the light of the world. A city that is set on an hill cannot be hid. Neither do men light a candle, and put it under a bushel, but on a candlestick; and it giveth light unto all that are in the house. Let your light so shine before men, that they may see your good works, and glorify your Father which is in heaven."—Matt. 5:14–16.

JESUS MADE both of these statements. He said, "I am the light of the world" and "Ye are the light of the world." There is no contradiction here. I look about me on a lovely day and say, "The sun is the light of the world." Then in the evening the sun goes down behind the western horizon and the moon comes out in her glory and I say, "The moon is the light of the world." There is no contradiction in those statements. The sun is the light of the world but the moon becomes the light of the world because the sun shines upon the moon.

A Christian Is the Light of the World, Too

Now, Jesus Christ is the light of the world, but a Christian becomes the light of the world when Jesus Christ shines into a Christian's heart.

I should like to stop in passing long enough to say that I have seen the moon in eclipse. I have watched her shine in her beauty and glory until a shadow came over her face. And they told me that a part of the world had come between the sun and the moon. I have seen eclipses in Christian lives, too. I have known men to shine in wonderful beauty for God until

164

they permitted the world to come between them and their Sun. It may be that somebody here tonight has experienced an eclipse. Over your sky the world has cast its shadow, and you are no longer what the Lord meant you to be when He said, "Ye are the light of the world."

Henry Drummond said, "The greatest proof of the Christian religion is a Christian." A Christian is the unanswerable argument to the reality of the Christian religion. If you want me to judge a civilization, show me the type of men and women that civilization will produce. You judged the civilization of Germany by the type of German soldier in the recent World War. You judged Japan by the type of Japanese soldiers who fought in the recent World War. You judge a civilization by the sort of people the civilization produces. You judge a school or college by the type of character the school or college turns out. You judge a god by the sort of life that god can produce.

Now the world, to some extent at least, judges Jesus Christ by the kind of lives we Christian people live. Somebody has said that every Christian is writing a gospel; he is writing a chapter day by day. What is the gospel according to you tonight? What kind of chapter did you write in your bible this past week? What sort of chapter are you going to write tomorrow? Remember, "Ye are the light of the world." "Let your light so shine before men, that they may see *your* good works, and glorify your Father which is in heaven."

A story was told of a blind man who went one night down a back alley with a lantern in his hand. Someone said, "Why do you carry that light? It doesn't do you any good."

He said, "Oh, yes, it does; it keeps other men from stumbling over me." If you Christian people do not carry your lanterns down the alley of life, men are going to stumble over you into everlasting night and everlasting ruin.

"Ye are the light of the world . . . Let your light so shine before men, that they may see your good works, and glorify your Father which is in heaven." Did you ever stop to think that is a command? Your Lord, whom you claim to love and trust, has commanded you. It is a command from God, and not to do it is to disobey God.

Did you ever stop to think of the fact that everything God ever created obeys His voice, except man? When this universe was wrapped in chaos and darkness, God said, "Let there be light." In obedience to His matchless voice the sun unveiled its face and the world was lighted. When Jesus Christ was on earth He looked for fruit on a fig tree and found none. He cursed it and in obedience to His matchless voice it withered and died. When out on tempest-tossed Galilee His disciples awoke Him and said, 'Master, we are in the midst of a storm,' in the dignity of His glory and power He said, 'Wind, cease blowing; water, be still.' They said, "What manner of man is this, that even the winds and the sea obey him!" (Matt. 8:27). The wind obeys Him. The sea obeys Him. The highest arch-angel and the tiniest insect on mother earth obey Him, but you do not obey Him. You disobey Him. He said, "Let your light shine," and you have not been letting it shine. He said, 'Ye are the light of the world; let that light shine before men,' and you have disobeyed God. Oh, may God move upon our hearts tonight and give us a sense of our responsibility and our obligation. God help us to obey His voice!

Did you ever stop to think about it: God created you for the purpose of letting your light shine before men. You are to take His light and give His light out into the darkness of this world.

When I was a boy in the country I heard an old-time, ultra-Calvinistic preacher say something that startled me very much. He looked out over the crowd and said: "God made some of you people to go to Hell. You will just have to go. There is no way out for you. God made you for Hell and you will just have to go to Hell when you die."

As a little country boy I said to myself, "If God made me to go to Hell, I want to go to Hell. I want to be what God has made me to be. That is my ambition in this world." Listen!

If God made me to go to Hell, such a thing as Hell would be an absurdity. Anything that does what God made it to do, is happy. God made the fish for the sea and the birds for the air. The fish play in the water and the birds sing in the air, but you put the fish in the air and the birds in the water and they die. God did not make fish for the air, and God did not make birds for the water. Anything in its place is happy; and if God had made men for Hell, the idea of a Hell would be an absurdity. God would change the flames of Hell into flames of matchless glory. Say, God made you to walk in the light as He is in the light that you might have fellowship with God and God might have fellowship with you. God made you for Heaven. Hell was made for the Devil and his angels, and if you go to Hell you will be an intruder. Say, God made Heaven for you. God made streets of gold for you! God made cloudless skies for you! God made the Holy City beyond the stars for you! And when you get to Hell, if you go to Hell, you will be an intruder. That is what makes Hell. All the agony and sorrow that you have on this earth come to you because you are out of your sphere, you are not where God wants you, you are not in fellowship with God.

Oh, I am so glad I can tell everybody that God wants to save them. I am so glad I can look into the face of every human being under the stars of Heaven and tell them that God loves them and Jesus died for them. I can go to the home of the rich man and listen in vain for my footfalls on carpeted floors; I can look at his beautiful pictures on magnificent walls; I can go to his table laden with the luxuries of life; I can sit beneath his gorgeous chandeliers of trembling crystal, blazing from the walls like bouquets of diamonds—then I can go out on a street corner and see a poor beggar who lifts his trembling hand and asks for a penny. If it were left to me I might say, "Come, ye rich man," or, "Come, ye poor man." But you leave it to Jesus. He looks down on the rich man's prosperity and the poor man's poverty and says, "Come, anybody. I'll take you. I would like to have you."

You may see in this city a manly, sober, moral, upright young man. He works hard all day and goes home at night to his little cottage where he is greeted by his loving wife and little children. Out yonder in the ditch is his drunken brother, a poor besotted wretch who staggers down a back alley with bloated face and bloodshot eyes to a cabin door to curse a ragged wife and hungry child. If it were left to you, you might say, "Come, ye moral man." But you leave it to Jesus. He looks down on the moral man's manhood and the drunkard's debauchery and says, "Come, anybody. I'll take you. I would like to have you."

You may see in this city a girl, pure, decent and refined. She has in her eyes the luster of purity, and the roses of modesty bloom in her cheeks. The most beautiful thing in the world is that kind of girl. But out yonder in an earthly hell is her fallen sister, a soiled dove of the underworld. She walks down the street with faded face and sad eyes. If it were left to you, you might say, "Come, ye girls of purity and respectability." But you leave it to Jesus. He puts His arms around this old world, locks His nail-pierced hands on the other side, hugs it to His bosom, warms it with His love and says, "Come, anybody. I'll take you; I would like to have you." Anybody in this country whom nobody else wants can be sure that Jesus wants him. You go hunt up the poor man and tell him that Jesus Christ would like to have him. "Ye are the light of the world." Say, let your light shine! Your life ought to be an invitation to everybody who sees you to come to Christ.

Now, let us go back to the first statement. Jesus said, "I am the light of the world." That is a marvelous statement. We read the things that Jesus said and just take them for granted. But think of somebody's living nearly two thousand years ago, walking the dusty roads of earth, standing in the darkness of the world, and saying, "I am the light of the world."

Jesus Is the Light of the Intellectual World

In the first place, Jesus is the light of the intellectual world. Jesus never wrote a book. As far as we know, He never wrote but one time, and nobody knows what He wrote then. But in spite of the fact that He never wrote a book, He is the light of the intellectual world. Woe be to those who leave Jesus Christ out of their scholarship! Listen to me, young people; for my philosophy of life I would rather sit at the feet of a woman who lives in a cabin and who can scarcely write her name but who knows Jesus, than to sit at the feet of the greatest scholar the world ever saw, if that scholar is not a Christian. "The world by wisdom knew not God" (I Cor. 1:21). You cannot think accurately unless you come to know Jesus.

Let me give you young people a little testimony. When I, was saved as a little country boy, eleven years old, we did not have such good schools. We did not have the advantages you have in the great schools of Chicago. I found Jesus in a little country church, and, you know, the next morning when I went back to school I had a real intellectual stimulation. I could understand things and see things that I had never understood nor seen before. Jesus not only comes into your heart when you are saved, but He also stimulates your faculties. He helps you to see. He lights up your intellectual sky. These men without God—don't you let them disturb you! Young people, don't you let the worldly-wise scholars who know not God disturb you. Poor, blind, weak, stumbling, ignorant men —how little they know!

Years ago I heard a story that impressed me very much and I would like to pass it on to you. In the city of Louisville, Kentucky, there lived a woman who had a parrot. She taught that parrot to say, "Good night," when she would put him in the cage at night and, "Good morning," when she would take him out of the cage in the morning. One day the bird got in a fight with a cat. The woman rescued the bird. That night she put the bird in the cage and said, "Good night, Polly."

The bird said, "Good night."

The next morning was a lovely spring morning. The lady went out to the cage and said, "Good morning, Polly."

The bird said, "Good night."

"Well," she said, "good morning, Polly."

The bird said, "Good night."

"Oh," she said, "but, Polly, what is the matter with you? Good morning!"

The bird said, "Good night."

"Well," she said, "Polly, don't you know when it is daylight? Good morning, Polly!"

The bird said, "Good night."

The woman got up near the cage and found that the birds eyes had been scratched out by the cat the day before. There were no more "Good mornings" for that poor, blind bird. O man without God, you cannot see! O Christless woman, you have no eyes! Jesus Christ is the light of the intellectual world.

Jesus Christ Is the Light of the Social World

Conditions are terrible in this world, but did you ever stop to think what they would have been had Jesus never come? Suppose there had never been a manger in Bethlehem. Suppose there had never been a cross at Calvary. Suppose there had never been an open sepulcher. Suppose there had never been a Sermon on the Mount. What a world it would have been! Everything worth having in this world came from Jesus. Jesus Christ made womanhood all it is in this country. In countries where His name is unknown women have always been slaves and burden-bearers. It was Jesus Christ who took the chains of slavery from the hands of woman. It was Jesus Christ who put woman on the throne and crowned her queen. Oh, I just do not see why all women and girls do not fall in love with Jesus. He is the best Friend women ever had. He is the Friend of all girls and all women. One of the saddest things in the world is that so many women and girls are turning the freedom that He bought for them into license to live wrong. He made womanhood all it is in the world!

Jesus Christ made childhood all it is in the world. Did you ever stop to think that no pagan writer ever said anything

about childhood's golden days? Childhood had no golden
days for a pagan.

Listen, young people, all the Christmas spirit came to you
from Jesus. It was Jesus who touched babyhood into beauty.
It was Jesus who was the first teacher to open His arms and
say, "Suffer the little children to come unto me, and forbid
them not: for of such is the kingdom of God" (Mark 10:14).
Little babies always fought to get into His arms.

Somebody else has said that Jesus is the God of little things.
He puts wings on archangels and He puts feathers on spar-
rows. He does not forget the little things. He puts all the re-
sources of nature back of the frailest flower that blooms.

Some time ago I was in Oregon, upon a mountain with
some friends of mine. I saw a little flower—I do not know
what kind of flower it was, but it was coming up through the
ice and the snow. The snow and ice had not melted, and that
little flower was trying to shake the ice out of its hair to get
up to the sun. This friend of mine said, "They never wait for
the ice and snow to melt. They always come up in the spring
like this before the ice and snow get away. They cannot wait
to get to the sun."

I said, "How much wiser those flowers are than some people I know! They walk away from the light and those flowers
climb up through the ice and snow to get to the light."

One morning down in Georgia I went for a walk and I
saw a little wild flower blooming in a little cluster of bushes.
It was a beautiful little thing. The little flower was lifting its
perfumed lips for the kiss of the morning. I stood there and
looked at it. I talked to it a little while. I said, "Little flower,
did you get lonely last night?"

The little flower said, "No; I never get lonely at night. God
keeps the stars awake to watch over me while I sleep."

I said, "Little flower, wouldn't you like to have some breakfast?"

The little flower said, "I have had my breakfast, thank you.
I draw my sustenance from soil and air."

I said, "But, little flower, you haven't dried your face."

The little flower said, "I never do that. I wait every morning for God's sun to dry my face."

I said, "Little flower, what do you do when you get thirsty?"

"Oh," it said, "I just tell God about it and God tells the sun to draw me a drink of water."

I said, "Little flower, what do you do when the sun gets hot?"

The little flower said, "Oh, I just tell God I'm too hot and God sends the winds through the forest to cool my cheek."

"Oh," I said, "little flower, I suppose I'm the only person who ever saw you; but you haven't bloomed in vain. Out here in this little spot where you are, you have talked to me about God. God is my Father."

Young people, never mind where God puts you; you shine where God puts you. I tell my boys and girls in Bob Jones University that the most important light in the home is not the chandelier in the parlor. The chandelier in the parlor is not used often, just when company comes. It is a beautiful light, more beautiful than the rest of them; but it is a company light. The most important light in your home is that little back hall light. It is not so bright. It does not light so much space around it, but it is kept burning all the time. And it is the most important light in the home. It keeps people from falling down and getting hurt. Listen! Maybe you are a little back hall light. Maybe you haven't much ability or much talent. Maybe God has hidden you away in a little secluded spot. Listen! Just shine for God where you are. That song, "Brighten the Corner Where You Are," is a wonderful song in its thought. Shine where you are! "Ye are the light of the world."

"I am the light of the world," too, says Jesus. He is the light of the intellectual world. He is the light of the social world.

Christ Is the Light of the Religious World

Religion is one thing and Christianity is another thing. Everybody has some kind of religion. Do you know what religion is? Get this and remember it: religion is reliance. The thing on which you rely for salvation is your religion, and your religion is no stronger than your reliance. A Christian is a person who, knowing that he cannot save himself, relies upon Jesus Christ and His atoning blood for salvation. That is my reliance.

The Christian religion is a religion of song. Atheists cannot write music. Pagans cannot sing sweetly. It is Jesus who puts a song in the heart. It is He who makes us sing. It is the sorrow of my life that I cannot sing. I cannot stay on pitch. I haven't a sense of pitch. But I have a song in my heart; I wish I could sing it. It is a song that I did not write. Jesus wrote it. He put it there in my heart Himself that night He saved me when I was eleven years old. Someday I am going to sing it. You have heard lovely music tonight, but you wait until you hear me sing! When I get to Heaven, that land of cloudless sky, I am going to dip my tongue in the melody of the sky, ask the heavenly orchestra to set the pitch for me, and I am going to sing that song that Jesus put in my heart.

Who else but a Christian can sing his way through the sorrows of life? Who else but a Christian could sing as Paul and Silas did, in a dismal dungeon when backs were lacerated and feet were in stocks? Who else but a Christian can go down into the valley of the shadow of death and say, "Glory to God! O death, where is thy sting; O grave, where is thy victory"? Who else but a Christian can see the coffin go down and say, "The Lord gave, and the Lord hath taken away; blessed be the name of the Lord." Oh, it is wonderful to have a religion that is a religion of light and song!

Jesus Christ May Become the Light of the Individual World

Did it ever occur to you that no two people really live in the same world? Everybody in this house lives in a little world of your own, a world of your own individuality, a world of your own peculiarity, a world of your own personality, a world where you hope, dream, and yearn and long—a little world all your own. You have things in your heart you just cannot tell anybody else. All music, all art, all the architecture, all human achievement is just a feeble effort of man to draw from his depths and get something out of his soul that he cannot tell.

My little grandson, Bobby III, was in my office some time ago. I said, "Bobby, some day Pop (he calls me 'Pop') will move out, if the Lord tarries, and your daddy will move in here. And you might move in his office, Bobby, and I want to be sure you are a Christian. Do you know Jesus, Bobby? Have you trusted Him?"

He said, "Yes, Pop, I've trusted Him."

I said, "Bobby, tell me how you know it."

He said, "Pop, it is so hard to tell—I can't get it out, you know. It is down there, but I just can't exactly tell it." Oh, listen: there is always something you cannot tell. There are unexplored depths. You can find the word, but it does not say all you feel.

I am talking to some woman tonight, or maybe some man, who is at the parting of the ways. And, by the way, don't you women get the idea that you have all the burdens. There are men in this house tonight with storms in our hearts that would sink all the ships at sea. I am talking to men tonight who have come to where the road parts. They look down this way and say, "I don't believe I can afford to go that way; that might lead me to disgrace. And this other road might lead me to defeat. I do not know what to do." I will tell you what to do: look up to Jesus! He will show you which way to go. Down yonder where it looked like disgrace, you will find honor. Where you thought it would be defeat, you will find victory.

I am talking to some woman here tonight who years ago locked up in your heart a secret sorrow. You threw away the key. You have spent all these years hoping nobody would ever know it. One day you thought you would tell somebody, but the moment you tried to you were ashamed to do it, and you said, "I'm never going to tell it. I am going to suffer

alone." Your dreams have faded, your hopes have been dashed
and you have gone through weary, lonely, sad hours alone.
Many times when everybody else has been asleep you have
stayed awake to weep. You poured out burning tears on your
pillow. The next morning maybe you heard the prattle of
little baby feet coming to the bed and you turned the pillow
over to hide your tears and began to smile. You do not know
what to do? I can tell you what to do. Trust Jesus Christ;
yield your life to Him. Listen, He will turn all those tears into
pearls, string them for you, put them in a crown of joy and
put the crown on your head. He will chase away the midnight
darkness. Oh, what a Saviour! There never was a cloud He
could not drive out of the sky.

He can drive the darkness out of the valley of the shadow
of death. Wait a minute! "Though I walk through the valley
of the shadow of death, I will fear no evil . . ." Listen!
Death is never a valley when a Christian gets there. It looks
like a valley on my journey there, but when I get there, death
is never a valley. You never knew a Christian who at the last
moment dreaded to die. He may dread it until the time comes.
He instinctively draws back. But you wait until he peeps
through the gate and sees what is on the other side!

Years ago there was a frail invalid woman, a lovely wife
who had a lovely husband. They had no children, and they
prayed that God would send them a baby. They kept praying
and kept praying. One day God sent a little baby into their
home. The little thing was there on the mother's arm, and
the doctor leaned over the bed and looked at the mother.
The husband and the nurse were there. The woman said,
"Doctor, am I dying?"

The doctor said, "Yes, dear. I am awfully sorry, dear; but
I must be honest with you. Yes, you are dying."

"Oh, doctor, I wanted this little baby so bad. Doctor, I
wouldn't mind dying if I could take my little baby along.
Can't I take my baby with me, doctor?"

The doctor said, "Dear, I'm awfully sorry. I'm awfully

sorry—I—I—am so sorry, but that little gate of death is so narrow that you will have to go alone. That is one gate you will have to go through alone. Everybody has to go through it alone. There is not room in that gate for even the wee little baby, so you will have to go all alone through the gate." Doctor, do not tell her that. Do not say that to her, doctor! You do not understand. She cannot take the baby; you are right about that. And her husband at the gate of death will have to say, "Good-by." That is all true. But I know somebody who can go through the gate of death with her. His name is Jesus. "Yea, though I walk through the valley of the shadow of death, I will fear no evil: for thou art with me." Oh, there is no dark valley to the Christian!

Years ago down South there was an old man dying, an old father. While he was dying his son stood at the bedside. His son had been to a university and had had his faith shattered. He watched his father dying and said, "Father, how does the valley look?"

The father said, "The valley?"

"Yes, how does the valley look?"

"What do you mean by the valley?"

"Why, Father, the doctor says you are in the valley of the shadow of death. And you have always talked about your faith and your Saviour and your religion. How does the valley look?"

The old man said, "The valley! The doctor says I am in the valley! Tell that doctor he does not know what he is talking about. Tell him I am not in the valley. Tell him I am on the sunlit summit. Tell him it is the brightest day I ever saw!"

Death for a Christian, I say again, may look like a valley as he journeys that way, but when he gets there it is not a valley. The light of the heavenly city floods the valley!

Christ, the Light of This Dark World

I remember years ago when I was a young man I was holding a campaign in a city. We had had only rain and mud and slush—I had not seen the sun in eight days. I had been under a strain. I was sitting on the front porch of a little frame hotel one Sunday morning. The vines had grown clear up beyond the second floor.

I looked up at the muddy clouds and said to myself, "It looks to me as if that great big sun could clear up the sky. Why can't you get rid of those clouds? You ought to be able to do it." While I was sitting there thinking I saw a great big cloud rent in twain and back of it was a misty veil. I sat there and watched that misty veil, shot through with holes of light. The great big sun stepped out from behind the cloud and waved at me, and I threw it a kiss.

I was carried back in my thoughts to the time two thousand years ago when midnight's blackest darkness hovered above this earth and wise men groped their way through the darkness, looking for light. One day a star appeared. That star led them across plains and mountains and rivers and over hills. And, like all true light, it led them to Jesus and began to shine over His cradle. That star did not go out at that cradle. That star was shining in the temple when He was twelve years of age and talked to the doctors. It was shining at Jordan when He was baptized. In His temptation in the wilderness, on the mountaintop, on the pinnacle of the temple, it was shining. It was shining in His miracles when He made the blind to see, the deaf to hear, the dumb to speak; when He cured the palsied, cleansed the leper, raised the dead.

One day the world said, "Let's put it out." The world does not want light. Its deeds are evil.

One time I called on a neighbor in my town just at twilight. The lady said, "Come in; Tom will be here in just a minute." I walked into the parlor and wondered why she did not turn the light on. It was getting dark and I sat there waiting for her husband to come. Suddenly her little boy came in and started to turn on the light. She said, "Don't turn on the light, Son; your mother's hair isn't combed."

Whenever Jesus came into a room He pressed the button.

Those old Pharisees said, "Cut off that light! We don't look right in the light." So the world said, "Let's get rid of His light," and they put Jesus on a cross. The heavens put on mourning and bowed to the earth to weep, the earth staggered under its load, and darkness settled down. It looked as if the light was gone. But wait a minute—maybe it isn't. Listen; a moment later the light flashed into the heart of the dying thief, got rid of all the darkness of his soul and got it ready to go Home to God.

Then they took Jesus down off the cross and put Him in a tomb. For three days there was darkness. Some of the disciples said, 'Let's go back to work.' Peter said, 'I'll go back to fishing. The light is all gone.' But three days later the star poured its light into the sepulcher. Some angels were flying around and that sepulcher looked so much like Heaven they thought they had got home, and they flew in!

Men and women, that star arose never to set. After a while the old world will catch fire and burn, and the moon, colored as red as blood, will hang her crimson livery upon the wing of the night, and the sun will drag up to the door of Heaven and refuse to shine. And breath from the nostrils of God will blot out the stars, and universal midnight will come. But there will be no midnight for a Christian. Heaven is a city of light.

Jesus, the Light of Eternal Heaven

John on the isle of Patmos, when the darkness of loneliness and the war of sorrow had settled upon him, got out his old prophetic telescope and said, 'I want to see what I can find up yonder where I am going to stay forever.' And he turned that telescope to the sky and looked through it. He said, 'It is a beautiful gate, isn't it? I never saw so much wealth! It is a solid pearl. And that wall! It is of jasper. Oh, the wealth! I want to see everything before night comes. I do not want to miss anything. If I am going to stay there some day, I want to look it over.'

Then he said, 'The streets are gold. They must have a lot of gold up there; they use it for pavement. And that river! I never saw any water as clear as that. It is as clear as crystal. And the tree—oh, what a tree! Oh, it is for the health of the nations.

'I must not miss anything because it is going to be night after a while. Before the sun goes down I would like to see everything in it that I can. What a city! Nobody is wearing mourning up there.'

Think of living in a city where nobody wears mourning! John did not see any wrinkled faces. The fingers of time had not pinched wrinkles around anybody's eyes. And no shoulders were drooping under the weight of their years. John did not see any little babies crying in pain. The saddest note I ever heard is the cry of a little baby who cries out in the night and cannot tell what hurts him. I want to live in a city where babies do not cry.

John said, 'I wonder where the graveyard is. I do not see any—oh, there is no death there!'

Then he said, 'I must see it all before night gets here.' He took hold of his telescope again and then he said, 'It is away past night-time—the days must be longer up there.' He kept looking and looking and looking, on through the hours and hours and hours; and it was just as bright after hours passed as it was when he first looked. And John cried out in matchless ecstasy, 'There is no night there! The sun never sets!'

Think of living in a city forever and forever where there were no graveyards, where nobody died, where no babies ever cried in pain, where nobody wore mourning! Think of it! Think of a city where there is no sin, a city where nobody ever dips his tongue in the slime of slander to try to ruin somebody's reputation. Think of it. Oh, that city is my home! There shadows never come. There evening twilight nor morning twilight ever comes—it is always noonday splendor. Oh, the glory of that city! And there are no tears there.

Dr. Len G. Broughton, the great southern preacher, told me a wonderful story. He said years ago in Virginia, just after he gave up medicine to become a preacher, he was pastor of a church, was having a very wonderful ministry and was very happy. But in his church there was an old bachelor, a refined, cultured gentleman. One day this bachelor said to Dr. Broughton, "I am of so little use to God. I am such a timid person; I just do not feel that I am any good at all. But I have been praying that God would show me something I could do for Jesus. I believe I have found something—I believe I would make a good usher. That is the only thing I can think of. If you will let me usher in the church, I believe I can do that for Jesus."

Dr. Broughton said, "I'll be so glad to do it." So he spoke to the chairman of the committee and the chairman said that he would like to have him do it. Everybody smiled about it, knowing how self-conscious and timid he was. But the next Sunday morning this refined, cultured gentleman came in his cutaway coat, his gray trousers, his patent leather shoes and his nice gloves. He ushered everybody down the aisle with such dignity. People never saw anything like it. Everybody looked at each other and smiled. I never saw anybody so radiantly happy. He was back that night. He was at prayer meeting. He did not miss a service. Weeks went by and he kept coming to every service. He was so happy—he felt that he had found something he could do for God."

Dr. Broughton said: "One day he got sick and the doctor said his condition was rather serious. I used to go to see him every day. One day I was on the way over there and I met the physician. The physician said, 'Dr. Broughton, Tom cannot possibly live through the day.'

"I said, 'Well, I knew he could not live.'

"As I went up the front steps his old mother came down to meet me and said, 'Dr. Broughton, I want you to ask my boy if he is ready to die.'

"I said, 'I know he is ready.'

"She said, 'Well, I know it, too; but you know I am his mother, and I just want him to say he is ready.'

"I said, 'Well, I'll ask him.'

"I went in and sat down by his bed and said, 'Tom, I want to read you a chapter out of the Bible. Tell me what to read.'

"He said, 'Dr. Broughton, there is one chapter in Revelation I have read every day since I've been sick. It is that chapter where it says He shall wipe away all tears. I hate to be a baby, but I had been of so little use to God until I began ushering. Since then I have been happy. I have felt that I was doing something for God. When time for a service would come and I could not be there I would cry. Then I would read that chapter where it says He will wipe away all tears.'

"I said, 'I will read it to you, Tom.' I read it and got down on my knees and had prayer. After I got up both of us went to crying. We were not crying because we were sad. God was there and our hearts were melted. A great big stream of tears would flow down each of Tom's cheeks and across the hectic consumptive flush. I stood there and looked at him. I had a big silk handkerchief in my pocket that had been given to me by a man uptown, which I hadn't even unfolded. But I took it and began to wipe his tears away. I kept trying to dry them, but I could not dry them as fast as they would come. After a while he said, 'I'm trying to stop, Doctor. I'm so happy!' I could not get them dried, and after a while the handkerchief was so saturated I just gave it up. He stopped for a minute, then a great big stream of tears flowed down each cheek. He smiled at me through his tears and said, 'Dr. Broughton, the next time they are dried, Jesus will do it.'

"I told him good-by. In about an hour or two they called me and said he was dead."

Oh, the tears, the burning tears on the cheeks of God's people! Some day Jesus Christ will take His nail-pierced hands and wipe them all away. I used to think my mother was pretty good about that, but nobody can dry them like Jesus!

And in that city you will never get tired. Everybody is tired. This is a weary world. You young people are tired. Everybody is tired. It is so strenuous to live now. Life is such a strain. The memory of my mother is the memory of a tired face. The only time that I ever saw her look rested was when they put her in her coffin and stretched her hands across her breast. She slept the sleep of death and she looked so rested that day. I do not know what people mean when they say they are rested. All my life I have been under a strain. The only time I can remember that I felt completely rested was a few years ago out in the middle of the Atlantic Ocean, coming back from Palestine. One day out at sea it suddenly occurred to me that I was not tired. Oh, you weary, tired bodies and tired minds and tired hearts! When you get to Heaven you can work all you want to and never get weary. There is no fatigue there, no weariness. Nobody gets tired there. Think of a Heaven like that. Oh, blessed be God, some of us are on the way. What a place it will be!

I have seen the vista of rolling hills and verdant valleys, of winding streams and forests with their changing colors. I have seen the sky on wintry nights bejeweled with countless stars. I have seen the hand of God sweep the eastern sky with the glory of a dawning day. I have seen Him put His canvas on the western horizon, dip His brush in fire, and paint the exquisite tints of golden sunsets. I have caught the odor that floats through park and tropical islands on summer evenings. I have heard the music of the organ, the piano, the violin as they have responded to the master's touch. I have heard the matchless music of the human voice. But all I have ever heard and dreamed and yearned for and hoped for cannot compare with the first rapture that will thrill my heart when I look within that city gate!

> I want to go there.
> I mean to go there.
> I intend to go there.
> I do.

　　　　I want to go there.
　　　　I mean to go there.
　　　　I intend to go there.
　　　　Don't you?

Christian, Let Your Light Shine

Will you let me take just two or three minutes to tell you a story and to exhort you a little? Listen, let's you and I let our lights shine down here. And then if Jesus tarries and calls us home, I am going to ask Him to let me sit in a window up in Heaven and pull up the shade a little and let a little light come down. There is so much darkness in the world.

Down South after the Civil War there was a widow whose husband had fallen in battle. Her fortune had been swept away. She was cultured and refined but she had never known what it meant to work. She had a little boy. After a while when starvation was staring her in the face, she went to the field to supervise her own farms. While she worked her little boy played in the hedge.

The little fellow grew up to be about twelve years of age. He said, "Mother, I'll take over the farms for you. You mustn't go any more." So the mother stayed at home and the boy took over the fields. He would go to the fields early in the morning and every evening just at twilight he would come home. He would come through a grove and there was one little place in the forest where he could look through the branches of the trees and see the light in the cottage window. That was the signal that everything was all right at home. After a step or two the trees would come in the way. He got in the habit as the days and months and years passed of stopping there and looking for the light.

One time he was coming home from the fields, but when he reached that spot and looked through the grove the light was not there. He went on quickly. He rushed to the house, struck a match and lighted the lamp on the table. There in the bed was his mother, cold and lifeless. He went over, put his arms around her, reached down and kissed her lips of clay. Near her head he saw an envelope. He opened it and read these words:

"My dear son,

"I have a feeling that some day you may come home from the field and the light may not be in the window of our home. I have a feeling that some day I may have to move that lamp and place it in Heaven's window. But, my boy, if you do come home some day and the light is not in the window, just remember I will have it in Heaven's window. Walk in that light and meet your mother some day."

Listen, fathers and mothers and young people, let us go home tonight and put lights in our windows, and let us keep those lights burning. And if Jesus tarries and we have to move, we will let them shine back. Death does not dim them. The lights are made brighter if they are carried through the valley of the shadow of death. They shine back into the other world.

When I was a country boy we had no good schools out there in the country, so my parents sent me away to high school, thirteen miles away. I was always a great mother's boy. I did not see how I could leave her. I used to stay at home and sit on the back steps and hold her hand and kiss her sweet face over and over. I remember when I got ready to leave for school. I was going to stay two weeks, and it seemed like such a long time. My mother came out to tell me good-by. You know how mothers are. She had some food packed in a box. She said, "Now, Son, you eat this in your room. You will be timid for the first two or three days and don't you go hungry." She kissed me good-by and said, "You are going away now. Be a good boy."

I went away. Then I came home and my mother met me at the gate and said, "Have you been a good boy?" And every time I ever left my mother—if it were for just one day or several hours—she would say, "Now, Son, you are going away; be a good boy." When I came back she would always ask me the same question, in the same tone of voice: "Have you been a good boy?"

One day I was going away to stay two weeks and she came out to tell me good-by. When she kissed me her lips were a little warm. She had a strange flush in her cheeks I had never seen before and a strange expression in her eyes that concerned me. She said, "You are going away, Son; be a good boy." I told her good-by and went off.

At the end of ten days I had an opportunity to go home. I got there at night. My father heard me drive up, so he came out to meet me. He said, "Son, I'm glad you have come; your mother is very sick. I was going to send for you tomorrow." That memorable night is before my mind tonight. Those fevered arms—I can feel them now as my mother put them around me, pulled me down to her, and kissed me and said, "Have you been a good boy?"

When I went home the next time there was no mother to go with me to the gate, no mother to kiss me good-by. There was no mother to tell me to be a good boy. But when I went home the next time I had a kiss I had never had before. It was Mother throwing me one from Heaven. And I saw a light that day, brighter than I had ever seen. It was Mother's lamp shining from the window in the sky. I heard a voice. It was Mother's voice and Mother's sigh, mingled with music that angels make on harps of gold. That voice was saying, "You are going away, Son; be a good boy."

Men and women, listen. You Christian people listen! Let's trim our lights and let them shine. What do you say? Some of us haven't much longer. Let's let them shine to lighten the pathway of men to God.

I am talking to somebody tonight whose mother prayed for you before she died. She is up in Heaven tonight. I am talking to somebody whose father is there. There is some man here whose wife has gone on, or maybe somebody whose child has gone on. The lights are shining back. And best of all, Jesus Christ is up there. They are with Him tonight in fellowship. You can come into the light, too. There is somebody here who has never known what the light means. You are living in darkness. You can come into the light tonight. God help you!

"Ye are the light of the world . . . Let your light so shine before men, that they may see your good works, and glorify your Father which is in Heaven." God send us out today to do His business!

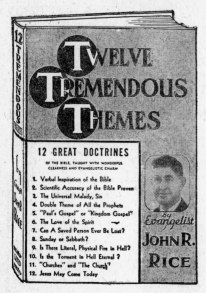